The Caretaker Monthly

Sharing the Journey

⌘

Jodie "Medicine Walker" Boxell

Bloomington, IN 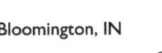  Milton Keynes, UK

AuthorHouse™
1663 Liberty Drive, Suite 200
Bloomington, IN 47403
www.authorhouse.com
Phone: 1-800-839-8640

AuthorHouse™ UK Ltd.
500 Avebury Boulevard
Central Milton Keynes, MK9 2BE
www.authorhouse.co.uk
Phone: 08001974150

First published by AuthorHouse 2/10/2006

ISBN: 1-4208-9126-X (e)
ISBN: 1-4208-8733-5 (sc)

Printed in the United States of America
Bloomington, Indiana

This book is printed on acid-free paper.

CONTENTS

Acknowledgements

⌘

Over many years I have watched my children grow and I have learned many things from them. I have watched them make many choices, some good and some not so good. The path that they have followed has been the way they chose to live their lives. I have children and grandchildren and I am very proud of the ways they have chosen, their path gives me honor but I must be humble in knowing it was their choice, not mine. I am thankful to my sons, Adam and Robert, and to my daughters Samantha and Jaymee, for teaching me about life.

There is one I owe my life to, my best friend, my confidant, the one who has guided my path for so long. The one that has pulled me from the pitfalls I have fallen into and forgiven me for the mistakes I have made. The one that listened to me for a quarter of a century while I released my passions and my aggravations about how the earth is treated. She is patient, she is kind and she is most of all, understanding. She is the highest point, the most wondrous view I have ever had the pleasure of seeing along my trail of life. I would never have written what I thought or felt had it not been for her, the Crane Woman, my wife, Maryann.

Introduction

⌘

This book was never intended to be a field guide but rather a source of food for thought. Although there is reference here on how to use some of the powers of the plant community and how to be comfortable with only the gifts the earth provides, there is the idea of acceptance and the attitude of thankfulness for what nature so freely gives.

There are so many people I meet that seem to think food is not fit for consumption unless it has been processed and canned or packaged. They also think that medicine has to be synthesized in a laboratory and formed into a pill or capsule to be effective. For many years, on many occasions, the earth has fed me , provided healing herbs to care for the maladies that sometimes afflict me, but mostly the earth has nourished my soul, quickened my spirit and made me realize just who and what I am.

Since mankind has came into being, there has been little if any change in his physiology nor have the attributes of the natural world given up their roles in the cycle of life. Mankind, on the other hand, has changed much in his way of thinking, what he considers socially acceptable has become a burden to so many when it comes to food and medicine. The human race, it seems, is constantly trying to separate itself from the natural world as if we are different from all of the other entities that exist on this planet. There is a reality that remains and will always be. What the earth provides for our lives has always been and there is nothing that can be added or taken away. The elements of our survival are given on a daily basis and our life depends upon how we treat those things that so often we take for granted.

When you look at the big picture, life on earth, there is more diversity, more intricacy of the way lives work together, more wonder and beauty than the mind can absorb. When looking at that big picture, there is a man, a woman and a child in it. They are not the center of the picture or by any means the main focus of it, just a part of it. They blend in with the rest of it, yet the picture would be lacking if they or any other part of it was missing.

I have spent my life wandering and wondering about all the things I see, smell, hear and touch. I have had the opportunity to see many places of wonder just because I chose to go there. I have experienced things that many never will simply because I was still. I have learned so much from the silent teachers yet I feel I have just begun. My life belongs to all those that make it possible, those things I know about and to those things I will never learn about or be able to understand.

For all that I have been given, what can I give in return?

Care.

THE CARETAKER MONTHLY

SHARING THE JOURNEY

JANUARY

⌘

January, the beginning of another year, at least in the way we have become accustomed to measuring time. For many, this is a time of reflection, plans and dreams of the year to come, resolutions of things we feel we need to change. A new year represents a new beginning, a fresh start, but why now? Because now, January is the period in the space of time that we have decided to label as the beginning of the year. In the cycles of nature there are many beginnings and endings. There is beauty in a circle as in the circle of the seasons where there is no end, just the continuing cycle of life. What is the start of the new year other than a label that has been tacked on to a space in time? What is that label anyway? It is an invention of man, a way to keep track of his or her affairs, a way to coordinate the many things that need to be accomplished within a given amount of, there's that word again, time. Time and the processes that take place in the course of it have been going on since, as far as we know, forever. All we have done is learned how to divide it into fragments for our own convenience. I hope the labels we have placed on those fragments of time will never be the downfall of our comfortable way of living that is so dependent on the technology that has made us slaves to the clock.

I stood by the Colorado River the other day, it was in the evening and darkness was making it's approach. It's a good time to be out, to be still and quiet, to hear and see the creatures that come out at night. I watched the sun cast shadows on the mountains as they seemed to change their shape and color. The more distant ones grew closer to me and then began to fade into the horizon that more closely surrounded me. Finally the last rays of the Sun melted away and left me with the sounds of the water percolating through the rocks and the night life that had emerged without noticing me standing there. It was as if I was a rock, or a tree or even dirt, just there and oblivious to the thought of yesterday or tomorrow or an hour ago. I was living in the now, the moment, absorbing everything around me, but my human nature is always with me. I have a tendency to survey my surroundings and ponder those things that are beyond me. The darkness fell in full around me and the stars appeared. I found myself gazing at the Big Dipper, a part of the constellation known as the great bear. It is a familiar friend, that on a clear night will point out the north star to me and give me assurance of direction whenever I might need it. The great bear has always been there in the same place whenever I have looked for it in the clear night sky for my whole life.

Polaris, or the north star, seems like something of unwavering permanence to us. It has been a stationary point of navigation for travelers for centuries, but how permanent is it? The cycles of nature are not confined to the earth alone. The earth itself is involved in natural processes far to great for us to see and that take to long for man, in his brief measure of existence, to record. Polaris, that glimmering spot in the night sky that generations have faithfully relied upon to show them direction has not always been the north star. At present, Polaris is always within one degree of true north, but that will change. We won't see it in our lifetimes but it will happen. About 2500 B.C. the north star was Thuban, and the people of that time were confident in finding that star in the same place, all the time and to them there must have been some comfort, some stability in always finding it there. In another 2000 years from now the most northerly star will be Alderaimin. 13000 years from now the north star will be Vega and another 13000 years from then it will again be Polaris. Old Mother Earth has a tendency to wobble a little bit on her axis, a process called lunisolar precession. Although it would seem that a cycle that takes that long to complete would have no effect on us or life as we know it, I have to wonder. How many atmospheric conditions and climatic changes that we consider to be the cause of many natural phenomenon are actually in themselves only the effect of a much greater cause. My heavens, the stirrings that come to a persons heart from just looking at a star.

My thoughts suddenly plummeted back to earth as I again became aware of those things close to me. The ice floating in the river crunched and groaned in it's attempt to cling to the fragile edges of the bank ice that had melted during the day. At this time of year there aren't the sounds of insects and frogs, but to one who is still, there is the activity of life, the processes of nature that have gone on for so long. An owl sat on a limb in an old cottonwood tree, patiently waiting for some slight movement or rustle from a mouse or vole on the ground. A beaver swims effortlessly up stream in the narrow channel of open water that remains, in search of some more succulent tips of willow or alder to add to his winter food cache before the ice closes in for the winter. There is a red fox up on the bank diligently sniffing and nosing through the grass for another tasty morsel to satisfy his appetite or to share with the mate he has found to raise another generation come spring. Although they all seem to conduct themselves on instinct and intuition, they know that preparation is the key to their survival. In the act of everyday living, the wild creatures are much busier than I am, constantly on the search for the necessities of life, resting only briefly when they feel the need, yet I envy them. No matter how busy they seem or how well they are prepared for the days to come, they live in the moment. Yesterday is gone and tomorrow hasn't come. What is important to them is now. We too can enjoy that luxury if we allow ourselves. A moment is nothing but another space in time. The amount of time is unimportant, a moment can be a minute or an eternity, it can be whatever you allow it to be. We all need practice now and then at breaking the shackles that bind us to the clock, and inhale life, if even just for a moment.

Every place I have been, whenever I look at a natural setting, there is a beauty about it, regardless of what kind of climate or terrain it might be, it has a beauty all it's own. Here in the Rocky Mountains it is easy to survey quite a large expanse from one vantage point. As I peer across seemingly undisturbed tracts of wilderness, the deep shadowed valleys and the towering snow covered peaks that have guarded those valleys for so many centuries, I realize just how small and vulnerable I am. If I really thought that I was all alone, the scene before me probably would not seem so beautiful and pristine but more like bleak and dismal, even hostile and threatening. Whenever I venture out I am always prepared for the unexpected. If for some reason I am faced with an unexpected lengthy stay, I can rely on some friends to help me be more comfortable.

Mullien is a natural friend that can serve a variety of needs. Mullien (Verbascum thapsus) can be found throughout most of the United States and is fond of dry, open sunny areas. Quite often growing along roadsides and in disturbed soil areas. As a biennial plant, it grows a rosette of soft, fuzzy leaves in it's first year. The leaves are covered with fine hairs that gives them the unique look and feel that makes Mullien so easily recognized. The second year it grows a tall and elegant flower stalk that can easily reach four or five feet in height. Mullien is a very powerful medicine that deserves much respect. It contains large amounts of mucilage which is a demulcent that soothes the mucous membranes, and an effective expectorant which makes it big medicine against congestion and other respiratory ailments such as asthma. The way I prefer to use Mullein is to put a palmful of leaves, fresh or dried, in a pan of water and bring it to a boil, then breath the vapors for relief of a runny nose or congestion. Before drinking the tea it needs to be strained to remove the fine hairs that could irritate the throat. The tea has a very mild and pleasing flavor and soothes the digestive tract while making the effects of breathing the vapors longer lasting. The American Indians would sometimes smoke the leaves for the relief of asthma or congestion. Mullien should only be used once a day as it is powerful medicine and can cause some discomfort if abused. The delicate little yellow flowers that are produced on a cylindrical spike atop the stalk can yield an oil that has been used for centuries to relieve earaches. The Indians would also use the mature seeds as a paralytic fish poison due to the ample concentrations of a substance called rotenone. Since the flower stalks are so tall they are easily seen above the snowy blanket of winter. These stalks are a welcome sight to the chilly traveler since they are an excellent spindle for a hand drill to nurture a fire to life. The hard outer shell and the softer inner pith seem to work very well in combination with a fireboard made of cottonwood or willow to produce the little coal that can provide so much comfort, or even save your life. With care, it can also work as the spindle for a bow drill which is a much easier way to start a fire. Both methods of course, do require a skill that can be mastered only with a lot of practice and patience. There are many survival guides and books that can show you the ancient art of fire making but practice is the key. In a survival situation, the knowledge won't help much without the skill to go along with it.

Thistles are also our friends. There are several different kinds of Thistles and they are common and easily recognized so I won't go into the different species and names. There are some with particular medicinal value such as Milk Thistle which is used in the treatment of liver ailments such as hepatitis, cirrhosis and liver poisoning like that which is caused by eating the death cap mushroom.

There is also the Star Thistle which is believed to have an antibiotic effect and is often used to reduce a fever. All of the Thistles share some common traits. They, like Mullien, grow a rosette of leaves the first year and a flower stalk in the second season. Again it is the tall stalks that makes a Thistle obvious in the winter. In the spring, the very young tender leaves are exceptionally palatable before the spines grow stiff and later in the year the young stalks, before they bloom, tastes a lot like celery. When the growing season has passed, there stands the stiff, brittle stalk that seems to be just the skeletal remains of a previous life, but there is some life left. Beneath that lifeless looking stalk is a tap root that is full of nutrients and tastes good too. Once the root is pulled or dug from the ground it can be scraped and eaten but you will find it rather stringy and fibrous. If you slice it up and boil it until it is tender, you might like it more than you do carrots, I know I do. Since Thistles like the same kind of habitat as Mullien, they are often found in the same proximity. Within that hard dry stalk there are some fairly strong fibers that can be used to make cordage. You may need some cord for constructing a shelter, setting a snare for a small animal or even just to replace a shoestring. The stalks of both of these friends in nature will also serve as good tinder for the life giving warmth of a fire.

I always encourage the proper and responsible use of our natural friends. Allowing the plant community to share it's powers can not be done in a haphazard way. Absolute identification is a must, the right attitude, a sense of giving back and of course some humility are essential to the life and survival of the habitat of mankind, Earth. I walk with you, not before you or behind you but as a part, beside you.

January Part 2
Tread lightly

Our habitat, that space or area that gives us life, that contains   everything necessary for us to exist. How big is it? The answer would depend on what you consider necessary for life. A basic definition of habitat would be, an area that contains enough food, water, shelter and space arranged in a manner to sustain the population that lives within that area. There are many things that contribute to a healthy habitat and help to determine how much space is needed to support all who live there. When it comes to wildlife and the plant community, there are continuing cycles that work to maintain a balance among all the different lives that call a given area home. Some people would like to think that man has no part in this natural scheme of balance and harmony but this couldn't be further from the truth. There are those that wish to separate themselves from the natural world and its splendor. They try to convince us all that we should stand back and leave it all alone, that nature should only be observed as if it was a picture on the wall. It seems like they have lost all sense of their connection to the big picture, the oneness and kinship that we share with all life.

The population of people on the earth has increased to the point that most of us don't need to share the duty of stewards of the land, but it is necessary that some of us do. A certain amount of mankind needs to remain in touch with their surroundings and make wise choices in the management of our resources lest all will suffer. Most living things are restricted to a certain kind of habitat that provides for its own specific personal needs, but not humans. We have managed to adapt to almost any environment which has allowed us to inhabit practically every space on earth. That is why we need to be so careful and responsible in the actions we take that affect each and every different kind of habitat on this planet. For those that don't agree with hunting, fishing, trapping, forestry or any other kind of resource management, they are entitled to their opinion, but I don't believe that it should try to be forced upon those who don't share it. There is definitely a need for some of us to be involved in helping to maintain a healthy balance in the outdoor community, and those of us that do, need to do so in an ethical, safe and responsible manner. Sound judgment has to be based on knowledge, so before an opinion is formed, a person needs to look at some facts.

In 1996, enough people in the state of Massachusetts voted to ban trapping in their state. In just three short years the beaver population had overgrown its available habitat and the result was millions of dollars worth of property damage, roads washed out and even casualties due to flooding. Now certain groups are conceiving many expensive and unreasonable ideas for controlling an exploding beaver population. Since 1998, Colorado is experiencing similar problems due to laws that have been introduced by emotion instead of logic and fact. Several years ago, the whitetail deer that lived in the Brown County State Park in Indiana had become so numerous that their habitat could not sustain them. The deer were on the verge of suffering from starvation and disease. The solution was to issue a controlled number of hunting permits and close the park to normal activity for a period of time so that hunters could safely harvest a predetermined number of animals. The result was a quick and humane return to a healthy, stable deer population within the park. There are many that view the act of hunting as cruel. I guess they haven't watched an animal starve to death or suffer a slow and agonizing death from disease and exposure because they refuse to leave their familiar home range which is rapidly being replaced with concrete and pavement. If more of us would choose to be a part of the natural scheme of things, to participate with nature instead of trying to manipulate it, to become educated, ethical tools in the hand of management, as members of the natural community, a more harmonious, healthy and secure balance would occur.

As human beings, our habitat is not limited, we are everywhere. We share space with every land dwelling creature on the planet and the acts and decisions of being the caretakers are not always easy or pretty, but they are necessary. The fact that a few must perish so the majority can be healthy is an undeniable fact of life in nature. We need to hold on to our sensitivity and compassion for wild things, but not be blinded by it as we strive to take good care of our habitat, the earth.

Our path should lead us to explore the hidden worlds of those creatures around us that sometimes seem so familiar, yet so mysterious. We need to look at their lives, how we cohabitate with them, how their lives affect ours and how we affect them. Hopefully a spark will ignite a desire to pay more attention to nature and the impact we can have. It is an individual and personal thing, the relationships that we share with the lives that dwell so close to us, but to often go unappreciated.

Tread lightly, speak softly and watch intently. We are surrounded by teachers from the sparrow to the bear.

FEBRUARY

⌘

Winter it seems, has us firmly held in its icy grip. If you live somewhere north of approximately the 27th or 28th latitude from the equator, carving out an existence in the wild without being prepared would prove to be very strenuous, or harrowing, or even deadly.

February was named after the Roman god Februus, which the Romans considered the god of purification. At least here in the Rockies it seems fitting since the landscape is mostly white. According to the Miami Indians` calendar, February is the month of the hunger moon, which also seems fitting if you are familiar with, or if you can imagine their lifestyle.

Since the dawn of man, few people have had the understanding, the reverence and the acceptance of natures ways as the American natives. They did not allow their elaborate culture, their customs and traditions to lure them into believing they were above all other living things or in any way superior to all they shared their existence with. They realized that like the animals, they had to prepare for the lean months, that if they were not strong and well, they might die. February was well regarded as the month of the hunger moon since it has been three long months since the hunting moon drifted over the night sky, and five months since the gathering moon and a time of plenty. There has been some time since fresh food was available, and hopefully the stocks of dried nuts, seeds, meat and fish have not perished and enough was stored away to sustain the tribe until the moon of the birds returning next month. Provided all is well, there has been much teaching of the young ones in the skills of using what the Great Spirit has provided, the skills they will need to do their share for the tribe and to carry them through to an old age.

It is hard for some of us to really comprehend what that kind of life would be like. In modern times, our demand for the provisions we need and the comforts we enjoy are met with a short trip to the grocery store or nearest convenience center. The most noticeable change in our lifestyle as the months and the seasons go by are the clothes we wear. Our diets are not really affected by the seasons and the way we travel may be slightly hampered upon occasion. It would appear that the quality of life that we enjoy has been vastly improved since the days of old, that the lifestyle of the American Indian would not be something to cherish or envy, but what do you consider quality of life? This is only an opinion, but it seems to me that this rapid paced, technological, modern world that we live in has caused us to lose some of the truly distinctive qualities of life as a whole. I can not be satisfied in just the fact that my belly is full and my house is warm. I can not simply exist, I must live. I need to know what its like upon occasion to be challenged, to be cold or hungry or scared, to be alive in just that moment and love it.

I remember a day in February, I was traveling in one of my favorite areas on snowshoes. I was in a place called Kinny creek heading for the confluence in the trail that leads over to the McQuery creek drainage. I was going up to gather some plant stalks for a class I would be instructing on the winter use of wild plants. As I was going along I noticed a beaver pond that had been drained in the early fall by a flash flood that washed out part of the dam. Some beavers had come back to take up residence and were cutting aspens a few yards up from the creek. I couldn't help but wonder why they had made a move at this time of year and how well they will do until the ice breaks up. One thing was obvious though, they will have more of a struggle than they would if they had an underwater den entrance and a food cache in front of it They also will be more vulnerable to their shy neighbor that I noticed on up the creek. As I shuffled along I became aware of that eerie feeling that I was not alone. I started looking at my back trail a little more often than usual and I guess my sense of awareness became a little more acute. I kept noticing slight movements out of the corner of my eye. The trail was easy to follow so I started watching more directly to the side as I strode over the soft and almost silent newly fallen snow hearing only the faint crunch of my snowshoes. Finally, I noticed my friend that was quietly keeping me company from a very short distance. At first I had no idea of the intent of the mountain lion that so skillfully followed my progress. Carrying only a knife to cut plants with, I felt very vulnerable and knew that at this moment I was definitely not at the top of the food chain. I removed my snowshoes and tied them to my back just in case this big tom managed to slip behind me. As I walked, I watched him slip from one hiding place to another. It became apparent that the cougar was more curious than interested in a meal. Finally I had the chance to turn and look at him directly so he knew that I was aware of his presence. He seemed a little disappointed that I had caught him in the act of following me. After he vanished, I think we were both satisfied, I know at least I was, and I reveled in the moment. To me, that was truly some quality living.

When we get wrapped up in this rapid, noisy, needed it yesterday, don't have time, world that we live in, we tend to ignore an awful lot of what surrounds us. We often need to tune certain things out or we might lose our sanity. We can't pay attention to every little thing in this busy, noisy world and so in turn lose some of the finer qualities of living. As we learn to ignore, it becomes progressive until we notice only what we intentionally home in on, we become unimpulsive and so much is missed. Even in today's hectic way of living, if we try, we are able to slow down, to notice the small things and those inner feelings, that sixth sense you didn't think you had. Every now and then, its a good idea to ignore what you usually pay attention to and pay attention to what you usually ignore. You may start to notice things in a different way, a new way. You will see things that have gone unnoticed for so long that they have almost been forgotten. Things that need to be appreciated and experiences that are remembered so the quality of life can be improved.

There is a time in our lives, when we are young, before we are consumed with the rigors of the pursuit of happiness, prosperity and peace of mind. A time when there was nothing wrong with losing track of time once in a while and being entertained, or amused at the simple things around us or being awe struck by the wonders of the natural world. Its a shame that our busy lives don't allow us to easily take the time for stopping and wondering, so we need to make the time. The more you do it the easier it becomes and you are better for doing it. This may not be the path to prosperity, but it will definitely make it easier to track down some happiness and peace of mind.

. This time of year is the prime time for boredom to set in, cabin fever, don't know what to do syndrome. You really don't need a particular reason to go outside, just go out. Take a good look around and see what plant parts are left above the ground or snow. You might surprise yourself at how many you can identify. What animals or birds have left their signature in the snow and what do you suppose they were doing. If you look closer you might unravel a mystery that would have gone unnoticed. There is a lack of outdoor activity in February so if nothing else you can enjoy some definite peace and quiet and serenity. This is a very good time for some reflection, to gain back some connection to your inner self, to try to listen to that sixth sense and to realize your kinship with Mother Nature. Maybe you would like to work on some skills such as gathering the plant stalks you need for making cordage or finding the right consistency of cottonwood or willow for starting a bow drill fire. One of my habits whenever I am out is constantly being observant of what is around to offer me material for a comfortable shelter and a good place to put one.

No matter what the season is, there are many things that nature has provided for our needs, whether it is something to go along with the provisions we already have or something to serve in an emergency, but if you are in the habit of being in a hurry and looking far ahead, you will miss those things that are close, or the experience of a rare encounter, the things that make life a cherished gift indeed.

Toward the end of February, in most of temperate North America, the trees that belong to the Poplar family will develop young leaf buds at the tips of their branches. The sticky red resin they are covered with is known as Balm of Gilead. There is a fragrance about it which is why it is used in some perfumes, but it is more highly regarded for its ability to soothe and heal. Balm of Gilead has been treasured for generations for its broad use in healing wounds and as an anti-inflammatory and is mentioned in Genesis, the first book of the Bible

Two of the most common and easily identified trees in North America that belong to the Poplar family and produce this resin are the Black Cottonwood and the Quaking Aspen. The Black Cottonwood can be found most commonly growing along river banks and wet areas up to 5000 feet, the Quaking Aspen however can be found growing up to the tree line in the mountains.

As the end of the month of the hunger moon draws near, the days grow increasingly longer. During the course of the longer sunny days, the leaf buds of the poplars become red with resin, especially on the lower branches. This is when you want to start collecting them to procure an ointment very similar to the Balm of Gilead that can be stored and used at a later date. Always be careful in the way you harvest. This is a gift so treat it accordingly, with respect and gratitude and humility in the respect that you did nothing to gain it, it is simply there for you. With the right attitude, you can have more than just medicine, you can have good medicine. In order to procure the tincture from the buds you must soak them in denatured alcohol to release the resin. The alcohol will evaporate and with patience you will have enough to treat several small injuries to prevent infection and speed the healing process. Don't let the alcohol completely dry up, the resin will separate from the buds and create a surface film. Collect this and keep it sealed in a small vile, preferably glass.

These buds of the poplar trees, along with the inner bark, also contain salicin which is the active ingredient in aspirin. If you have adverse reactions to aspirin then you should avoid using any part of a Poplar tree or Willow or Alder. The buds and cambium of these trees also contain a considerable amount of vitamin C but have an extremely bitter taste because of the salicin. It can be consumed if the need for nourishment overrides the taste. Because of the salicin content, the buds or inner bark can be chewed on to relieve a headache or toothache or you can brew a tea which you can drink or use the same as you would the Balm of Gilead.

There are so many gifts that are offered by the earth. A gift should not be ignored but accepted with gratitude and respect. Taking a gift is not selfish or greedy to a thankful heart, it only acts to build the bond of a relationship. Until the birds return, go kindle a friendship.

February Part 2
Little friends of the high country

The picturesque views of the Rocky Mountains have a tendency to conjure up thoughts of the past, mountain men following the seemingly endless patterns of streams and beaver ponds that were laced through every valley and draw they came to. There were Indians that made their homes there, at least seasonally, and traversed the length of the ridges in pursuit of game and caught fish from the cold, clear waters of the mountain streams. The mountains have a way of capturing our thoughts and senses in places of serenity and with sights of grandeur that make us want to be there and experience the kind of habitat that gave birth to so much lore and so many legends. In the not so distant past, the dead of winter would find the presence of man almost nonexistent, even the Elk and Mule Deer had migrated into the plains because of the extremely harsh conditions that had descended on the high country. In the fall of 1805, as Lewis and Clark and the Corp of Discovery ascended the mountains, they found game scarce. An Elk or a Buffalo was nearly impossible to find and Mule Deer were as scarce as hens teeth. Only because of the infringement of mankind do the Elk and Deer stay in the high country year round, the Elk in particular were a plains animal until they were forced to change their habits.

The high mountain areas can be divided into several different smaller habitats and different members of the wildlife community can be found living in each one of them. There is a little creature called the Pika that spends its entire life above the timber line. The Pika is a small animal that is related to rabbits and hares. It has small rounded ears and rarely grows as large as twelve inches long. These interesting little folks have a very busy but short life. They live for only one to three years and give birth to their young two to three times a year. Most of their lives are spent beneath the heavy snowy blanket that covers their domain for nine or ten months out of the year. During the very brief summer season they gather plant material from the short grasses, moss and lichens that grow among the rocks and dry it in the sun to make hay to sustain them through their long stay among the rocks, beneath the snow, protected from the deadly elements on the surface.

Another one of our little friends that prefers to spend most of its time above the tree line is the Ptarmigan. During the warmer months, the Ptarmigan can be found almost exclusively above timber line, which is generally about 11,500 feet above sea level. As the winter months approach, their brownish summer plumage molts to a thick, white winter plumage that not only protects them from severely cold temperatures but also enables them to blend into the white landscape. The feathers that grow on their feet serve as natural snowshoes that allow them to stay on top of the soft, powdery snow that covers their entire winter habitat. The ptarmigans' diet is made up of seeds and buds and various plant parts that, however sparse, can be found within the realm of their preferred living area. They manage to find food and shelter by burrowing into the snow. In the spring, the male and female will choose a single mate after which the female will incubate the eggs in a barely discernible depression in the ground while the male remains gallant in his attempt to guard the nest from predators and then helps in rearing the young. The ptarmigan is an elegant creature with an impressive ability to thrive in such meager surroundings.

As we travel further down the mountainside, we enter into a different and at least to us, a more comfortable and familiar surrounding. We are greeted by the fir trees, the pines and junipers. This is home to a more familiar friend, the Snowshoe Rabbit. The name rabbit is used in a very broad sense. The snowshoe is not actually a rabbit but rather a hare, the difference being that a rabbit bears young that are hairless, blind and helpless in an underground nest. The hare builds no nest and gives birth to young that are fully furred and have their eyes wide open ready to learn how to fare for themselves. The snowshoe rabbit is sometimes more appropriately referred to as the varying hare. With each coming winter it sheds its brown camouflage to don a snow white coat of thick insulating fur. Although most members of the hare family seem to like the open, grassy areas, the snowshoe is one who prefers a thicker, more wooded home site. The thick fur that grows on its hind feet and enable it to travel over the soft snow, of course is what gave the snowshoe hare its name. Regardless of several feet of snow that covers this hares winter home, it manages to find enough to eat among the grasses that are exposed on the breezier slopes and from the bark of pines and aspen trees and from the buds of low branches. The snowshoe hare is naturally designed for its environment and so is a master at survival.

If we keep troding on down the slope, we will notice again the trees as they start to thin out into patches of sagebrush. These patches become larger and more widespread as we get closer to a river valley or a broad creek bottom and our view has expanded to a wider horizon of the distant mountain peaks and the landscape spreads out for miles before us. If we keep a close eye on the landscape, we will probably catch sight of a speeding jackrabbit as he quickly measures a more comfortable distance between him and the unknown visitors. On the other hand, we might be startled as one explodes from an undetected hiding place practically under our feet. Here again we have a case of mistaken identity since the jackrabbit is not really a rabbit but instead, a hare. Like his cousin the snowshoe, he has a white fur coat for the winter. Although he doesn't have the luxurious foot covering like the snowshoe hare, his feet are adequate to propel him across the countryside for incredible distances. The jackrabbit is more true to form for being a hare in that he prefers the more open areas. Even though he is usually found at a slightly lower altitude, he is still faced with finding food and cover on a landscape that is covered with snow. One advantage to the jackrabbits habitat is that there are more windswept areas that expose at least the upper portions of the grasses that often grow in profusion in the open, especially around the groves of aspen trees that spot the landscape. Upon a few occasions, I have managed to approach within an arms length of a jackrabbit and I am intrigued with their hazel eyes with an elliptical pupil. I also enjoy the way they lie there, motionless, apparently confident in their speed and agility, and their ability to escape should they feel the need.

All of the wild creatures we encounter have something to share with us, whether it's their lives they give for our nourishment, a lesson in survival and fortitude or even a shot of humility, they deserve our respect because just by the act of living, because we have all been given the gift of life, we all share a common thread. Life, it has been given to us so we can pass it on.

March

⌘

March, as referred to by the calendar of Indians in most of America, is the moon of the birds returning. The resonating sound of the Canadian Geese catch your attention and you look toward the sky to see the V formation of flight that trails off behind the lead goose as they make the arduous migration back to familiar breeding grounds. The lengthening days of March have triggered an ancient and irresistible urge in all migrating birds to return to their birthplace, or at least close to it, and rear their young to guarantee the survival of their species. In some places, close to the flyways, the skies become almost darkened with the annual flight of Geese, Ducks, Swans, Cranes and Herons. It is an awe inspiring sight and very good medicine for it signals the end of the lean months and the arrival of spring with all its blessings.

Different cultures have looked at the cycles of the seasons in different ways. In ancient Rome for instance, March was the first month and was named after Mars, the Roman god of vegetation that later became the god of war yet still marked the beginning of the planting season. With the adoption of the Gregorian calendar in 1582, the first month became January. Mother Nature however, pays no regard to what man decides to call the first or last, or where he chooses to place a month or a season on his time line.

The American natives seemed to understand this and so didn't necessarily designate a first or last month of the year but recognized the continuing cycle of the seasons as a circle in which there is no beginning or end but just a continuation of what has always been, that over which man has no power.

In the moon of the birds returning, with each rotation of the earth, our period of daylight increases.

The time of the sun shining on the face of the Great Mother Spirit becomes longer each day. Much more than the yearly average, in fact, we will gain about three minutes of daylight each day through the month, even as we pass the vernal equinox. The equinox is a natural occurrence that takes place twice a year, once in the spring called the vernal equinox and then in the fall which is the autumnal equinox. At both of these times, the periods of daylight and darkness are of equal length everywhere on earth. If you can picture the plane of the equator reaching out into space then you can see what is referred to as the celestial equator. Now the axis on which the earth rotates is not vertical to its orbit around the sun so if you can visualize the plane of the earth's orbit spreading out into the solar system to where it touches the sun, then you have another huge circle called the ecliptic. This is the path followed by the sun if you were able to watch it through the year against the background of space. An equinox is when the sun, in its path along the ecliptic, travels across the celestial equator. In the spring, the sun is moving from south to north across the equator and in the fall, he returns again from the north. The vernal, or spring equinox usually falls on the twenty first day of the moon of the birds returning and then the hours of day will outweigh the length of night.

The lengthening of days has yet another effect on the inhabitants of this marvelous planet we call home. The reaction that many plants and animals have to the increasing length of daylight in the spring and the loss of daytime in the fall is called, photoperiodism. It is probable that the fuse that lit the migratory frenzy among the waterfowl is this very thing. Another wild bird that can cause quite a stir is the wild turkey with his raucous gobbles that add an eerie tone to the quiet and serene early morning woods as he attempts to attract his lady friends to watch his ballet of strutting and pirouetting in all his grandeur. In the spring time he is, in my eyes, the monarch of the woods as he carries on with his elaborate courtship display. On the other side of the scale is the tiny hummingbird. Out of the hundreds of species of hummingbirds, the only one that breeds in eastern North America is the Ruby Throated hummingbird. There are twelve species that raise their broods in the western United States, and the Rufus that will travel as far north to breed as southern Alaska. All of the hummingbirds that breed in North America spend their winters in the tropics and then migrate to places that range from the deserts to alpine regions as high as sixteen thousand feet. As the days begin to rapidly lengthen, the Ruby Throated hummingbird prepares for the long trip ahead by storing up body fat that will increase his body weight by 50%. Cued by instinct and probably photoperiodism, they embark on a five hundred mile, nocturnal flight across the Gulf of Mexico. During this non stop ten hour flight, while producing as many as eighty wing beats per second, the hummingbird will use up just a little more than one gram of the body fat that had been stored up for the long journey. I am constantly amazed at the tiny things in Mother Nature that can perform in ways that seem so big and monumental.

Here in the high country, The first days of March don't seem to present a picture of spring. The surrounding mountains and mesas are still pretty much covered with snow. At lower elevations and on the front range which is the easterly face of the Rockies, there are beginning to emerge some very faint and generally unnoticed signs of the coming spring. March can be a time of unpredictable weather and what we humans might call Mother Natures` irrational behavior. What I notice is the sun making its brilliant appearance a little earlier in the morning, and the smell in the air. I don't know what it is except that it smells like spring. I have a tendency to relish the beginning of each season for I know there is a limit to how many I will have the joy of experiencing. If I live to be the average age of seventy five years old, that is how many times I will be blessed with witnessing each new season, and I am exceedingly grateful.

As you wander about the woods and fields, or the plateaus and ridges, the evidence of the approaching spring season goes very much unnoticed. The miracles of life that are taking place all around us seem to do so with secrecy, to gain a sort of momentum so that in time, spring can burst wide open in all its glory and make the land appear new and refreshed. With the longer days beginning to warm the face of the earth, the sap begins to rise in the trees, up from the roots, through the cambium layer of the bark to the tips of each and every living branch. The buds at the tips of those branches begin to swell until the tiny developing leaves emerge and the tree again, after the dormancy of winter, begins to breath. The roots of perennial plants are absorbing the moisture from the soil as the icy grip of winter is loosened by the suns warming rays. The roots are swelling and are full of the starches that have been stored for the energy it will need to go full cycle in one short growing season. As the surface soil warms, seeds that were fortunate enough to fall in an opportune spot will start to reach out with the first little rootlet that will eventually become a beautiful dainty flower or the foundation that anchors a mighty, towering tree to the earth and in turn becomes home to many others.

Spring is a very busy time for Mother Earth. The more we observe and the closer we look the more intrigued we become and with a caring attitude in mind, since we are the stewards of all that is natural, we can have a spring within ourselves. Perhaps the sap of humility will begin to rise in our veins and burst into the foliage of inspiration, if so, that ancient root that so firmly bonds us to the earth will grow stronger and we can more easily share what has been so graciously given. Life.

As the waning days of March grow closer, the signs of spring become more evident. Where the ice has given way to open water you can watch the waterfowl as they feed on debris that has been kept in natures freezer until their return. Upon occasion there seems to be a flurry of activity among our feathered friends as they scramble to claim the most ideal nesting spots.

As we meander up from the waters edge in to dryer areas and disturbed soil and open areas, we will find someone that has provided many tasty salads and helpings of cooked greens, Field Pennycress.

This nourishing little member of the mustard family grows wild throughout most of North America. Also known as one of the pepper grasses, it resembles some of its cousins, especially when it goes to seed, such as Shepherds Purse and Field Cress. Since Field Pennycress belongs to the Mustard family, it will have a certain bite or bitterness to it which can be more or less depending on the soil it grows in. I have become quite familiar with this little friend over the years and can tell by tasting a fresh leaf if it will be bitter or mild when cooked. This can also be a matter of preference or acquired taste. Quite often, what I think is palatable is too strong or bitter for my company so I need to tone it down a little by cooking it in two or three changes of water for about fifteen minutes at a time. I will admit that the fresh leaves have too much of a bite to make a salad from them alone but they add a pleasing flavor when mixed with milder greens such as Dandelion or the young stalks of Cattail. There have been several times when I have gathered Field Pennycress by brushing the snow from the basal rosette of leaves that develop much earlier than most annuals. It is my opinion that this short term blanching effect caused by the occasional spring sleet or snowfall tones down the characteristic bitterness and adds a crispiness to the young leaves.

Plant identification is critical so get some good field references before you go out to enjoy natures bounty and remember that Caretaker attitude, treat the land as if it were your garden and it will be for many years to come.

March Part 2
From the burrow

Spring is quickly approaching, the days are rapidly becoming longer, the earth has reached that point in her orbit around the sun where the northern hemisphere has gained the attention of the great fiery giant. The arctic regions are now beginning to experience their biannual sequence of day and night as they emerge from the darkness of the winter months into the continual daylight of summer. The warming temperatures and the longer days trigger some mysterious happenings that have to do with the cyclic affairs of Mother Nature, many of which may never be understood by scientists. The cold and harsh winter environment that exists in most of North America makes it impossible for some of its inhabitants to live, so Mother Nature endowed them with a unique tool to get them through the lean months, hibernation. During this month, those that have spent the winter in the deep slumber of hibernation, nestled in their den or burrow will awaken and emerge to greet another season of renewal.

In preparing for hibernation, the animal will spend most of its time eating to store body fat that will be its only source of sustenance for its long winter nap. Only when told by its internal clock will it settle in to the cozy place it has made and drift off, oblivious to the cold whipping winds above it until it is brought back to attention by the sounding of that internal time piece again in the spring. When going into hibernation, the animals body temperature lowers and the heart rate slows as a means of conserving energy. The spring awakening is brought on by an explosive release of body heat that is produced by the leftover brown fat and the muscles along with a quickening heartbeat.

Although animals that hibernate seem to have their own internal way of keeping time, it doesn't coincide with the same accuracy of time measurement used by modern man. Animals have never become slaves to the clock like we have. Their lives are not governed by the constant and monotonous ticking of each minute and hour but are synchronized with the gentle rhythm of nature. Animals that have been kept in captivity, under artificial and constant conditions for extended periods of time, have been known to fall out of sync with their natural winter and start to hibernate in the spring or even summer. The conditions of the seasons always vary at least a little. When it comes to timing, there are few absolutes in the realm of nature, so for those lives that depend solely upon Mother Nature, all that they do must be in harmony with their habitat and environment so their contribution to nature is not diminished.

There are several members of the wildlife community that spend their winters in hibernation but not all go into a deep state of dormancy. Some, like the pika, even store food in their burrows and can be fairly active in their dark and secluded winter home. Others, such as the bears and marmots do fall into the state of slumber that most of us associate with hibernation.

Marmots can be found over much of the North American continent. From the Atlantic coast to the Mississippi Valley, in Canada and even as far north as Alaska, this species and subspecies of Marmots are referred to as Groundhogs or Woodchucks. In the west there is another specie called the Hoary Marmot. When the adult female emerges from her den and hibernation, generally around mid March, she is already bearing the young that she will give birth to this spring. The male had awakened last month and left his den to make a less than gentlemanly visit to breed with his mate while she slept and then returned to his den and again, into hibernation. Groundhogs are strong diggers and normally excavate their own den which can be somewhat elaborate and contain several compartments. It usually has more than one entrance. The main entrance is quite conspicuous since all the dirt from digging forms a sizable mound in front of the hole, but the other hole can sometimes be difficult to find because it was dug from the inside and emerged in a concealed spot which was the very intent of the builder.

Imagine that you are a Coyote or a Bobcat and you have spied a feeding Groundhog at a distance and you are, as yet, undetected. You begin your stalk, keeping the brush and tall grass between you and your anticipated meal. You move closer, stealthily, inch by inch, freezing whenever your quarry looks up. You can see the entrance to the Groundhogs` den and plan your approach so as to head it off when you make the final dash. You are finally there, you are crouched with your feet directly under you, your claws have curled into the firm earth and you are ready for the race to the den. The Groundhog senses something, it stands straight up and you can feel it, the moment of truth, eye contact! The rodent drops to its feet to run, you launch yourself into a burst of speed toward the path between your meal and its den but the Groundhog didn't go that way, you change course, losing momentum and your meal disappears, somehow it just vanished. You go over to where you last saw it and there, in the tall grass, under some brush is another hole, a flat inconspicuous one.

You can hear and smell the Groundhog, just below the surface but out of reach and safe within its underground fortress. Maybe if you keep snooping around you can find a mouse, or a vole, or at least something easier to catch.

When a marmot senses danger from a distance, or sees something within its domain that it doesn't particularly like, it emits a loud, shrill whistle by which it has gained the nickname "Whistle Pig". The length of their whistle can vary from a very short one to three or four seconds and will alert any other Whistle Pig in the vicinity. When one hears the whistle of another, it will usually stand up to gain a better view of its territory. As a boy, growing up in Indiana, I would whistle to make them stand up so I could spot them from a distance and then stalk close enough to collect one with my 22 rifle. They make excellent table fare especially when they are in their first year. Some people will turn their nose up at the idea of eating a Groundhog yet will go in pursuit of a rabbit which also lives in a hole in the ground, is a vegetarian and has buck teeth.

Where I live now, high in the Rockies of Colorado, there is a close cousin to the Groundhog, the Hoary Marmot. Up here we call them Rock Chucks. Their lives and habits are the same as their lowland cousin, but their habitat is much different. They don't have the soft soil of the eastern woodlands to burrow into, but they burrow just the same. One of the big differences that I have noticed is that quite often, they don't have that concealed back door entrance, or escape hatch for when the need arises. The Rock Chucks seem to always be on a steep and open rocky slope that affords them a superior vantage point over their domain. Maybe that is one of the reasons they don't always often have a second hole, along with the fact that in the process of digging, they must maneuver their way around many immovable rocks and boulders. I would imagine they often have to abandon an avenue into the mountainside to seek a different way around. I see them quite a lot just laying on top of a rock, soaking up the sun and peering out over a vast landscape. When a predator slips up on a Hoary Marmot and catches it unaware, it is a feat of monumental proportion. The Rock Chuck, I believe, has better vision than the Wood Chuck and can define an object at longer distances. When they voice their warning cry, it is much shorter than that of the Groundhog, it sounds more like a loud, high pitched peep, but it gets everyone's attention just the same and you see little Marmot people standing up, scattered across the mountainside, and nothing goes undetected.

When the Marmots come out, you know that spring is in full swing and natures storehouse is in the process of being restocked. It's a time of regrowth, rebirth and refreshment on the face of the great Mother Spirit, and the cycle continues. Watch and listen to the teachers, and be grateful.

APRIL

⌘

The hunger moon is well behind us now, the moon of the birds returning has blessed the people, now is the time of the green grass moon, April. The air is filled with the sound of singing birds. The dawn is announced just as the first hint of light appears on the horizon by the voice of the Wild Turkey gobbler as it echoes from his roost in the creek bottom. If you listen closely you may hear the drumming of a Ruffled Grouse. In the high country, you might detect the cluck and drum of a Blue Grouse in his attempt to attract an interested female. By hearing the subtle mating call of this high country dweller, you can be assured that you are very close to him, so if you stay quiet and still, you could have the opportunity to watch him dance to his very own love song. Now as we wander out of the cover of the timber and into the open, onto the mesa that is strewn with sagebrush and the first emerging shoots of the green grass, we might catch sight of a Sage Grouse or maybe a Sharp Tailed Grouse as they carry on with their elegant courtship display before a gathering of their suitors. The spirit of the Earth Mother has awakened from her long rest and is refreshed, the season of renewal is at hand and the miracles of life let themselves be known. The herbs and grasses stretch forth to begin the process of making food and medicine through photosynthesis as only they can do.

The birds and animals prepare to raise their young and instill in them all that is necessary for life in the wilds. The buds that have swollen at the tips of the trees branches are bursting with the foliage that will shade the earth from the heat of the sun. The workings of Mother Nature are well under way.

On a clear night, as we gaze at the heavens, there is an old and familiar friend hovering in the north part of the night sky, the constellation of the Great Bear, also called Ursa Major or more commonly known as the Big Dipper. The Great Bear has been a friend to many for a long time since he points the way to the north star, who is named Polaris. By mid April, the Great Bear will have reached his highest point in the night sky which could be taken to represent the beginning of another cycle in its journey around the circle of life.

With the thought of April, I am often reminded of the old cliché " April showers bring May flowers" which is usually true. When we say or hear that old phrase, what we picture in our minds eye is more than likely, not snow showers.

Here in the high country of the Rocky Mountains, near the door post of the Great Spirit, there is nothing surprising about snow falling during the green grass moon. In the valleys, much of the winter snows have departed and revealed the rich and moistened face of the land. These snow showers do not remain for long but quickly melt back into the earth to nourish it, they are only the fading breath of old man winter. To me, a white April shower is a welcome sight because of the short term blanching effect it has on some of the young and fresh herbs that grace my families dinner table. Many times, I have brushed away the new fallen snow to reveal a crispier and milder tasting morsel to gather and take home for a refreshing salad or a cooked green to go along with the fresh trout that came from the newly opened waters of spring. These new and fresh greens are much appreciated since they are so seasonal and can be enjoyed in this way only at this time of year.

There are many members of the Mustard family that grow in various habitats scattered throughout North America. In the higher elevations, there are several, such as Field Pennycress and Shepherds Purse, there are also a couple that I don't consider quite as palatable like Tansy Mustard and Hedge Mustard.

These same friends can be found growing in much of North America and southern Canada. At the lower elevations, mostly from the front range of the Rockies and east, thrive some other very delectable members of this plant family such as Wintercress which I have greatly enjoyed many times. There are also the traditional mustards, Black Mustard and White Mustard, both of which have been cultivated in gardens and are enjoyed by many. As you are out identifying and gathering these tasty early risers, don't forget to meet the prolific Garlic Mustard. Its flavor explains its name, but not offensively. Garlic Mustard can add a pleasant flavor to a salad when mixed in with some blander tasting greens or is very good as a cooked green. Perhaps you prefer your greens to be a little milder, if so, you can cook them in one or two changes of water.

In the days of old in North America, when the people lived entirely off of what the land provided for them, I can only imagine how grateful they were for the moon of the green grass. After living all the way through the lean months on the dried foods they had preserved in the fall and making it past the hunger moon. After months of pounded grain, dried meat, stored roots and pemmican, the fresh, green and leafy vegetables most surely were relished with many prayers and thanksgiving.

In this day and age, our existence is not nearly as hard to maintain as it was for the American Indians. Our future and our survival is not threatened by the harsh winter environment. Our diets are not affected by the seasons and the foods we enjoy most are available to us at all times of the year, so we can never experience the feelings of the people of the earth in the spring time, when natures bounty once again secured them and their hopes and dreams revived.

By observing the workings of the natural world around us, by quietly watching and listening to the teachers with an open heart, we can again begin to recognize that ancient link that lingers deep within us that ties us to the earth and the forces of nature. As we become familiar with the faces of our wild friends and learn to accept what they give, even though it is simply a desire to learn, that age old bond becomes stronger and we will find something we weren't searching for. We will learn how to give back.

April   Part 2
The colors of spring

As the days pass through the month of the green grass moon, the Grandmother spirit is preparing to adorn herself with the many colors that will splash across the land. Colors that will grow and fade and continually change as the summer and autumn months drift by. April has not yet graced us with the warm colors that accent a season of plenty but the evidence of its coming is in the new, green shoots that are rapidly rising above the decaying remains of the last growing season. Although the landscape is not yet covered with the colors and beauty that usher in the planting moon, there are splendid views indeed to behold , if we were to look beyond the surface, or venture past the edges of what we view from a distance.

Mid April is when the Rainbow Trout will answer the calling of the Great Mother Spirit and be stricken with an urge, natural to all living things, to propagate, to insure the survival of their species. The Rainbow Trout is a native to almost the entire length of the North American Pacific coast. Since it is one of the most popular game fishes in America, it has been successfully introduced in most of the United States except for some more southern states. The Rainbow is a popular fish because of its strength while doing battle with an angler and for its exceptionally tasty flesh. In the Rocky Mountains, This well known member of the Trout family will begin to spawn about the middle of April, when the constellation of the Great Bear is at its highest annual point in the night sky. The Rainbow Trout wears a coat of many colors, generally with a green back and tail that can vary in shades according to the habitat, a pink strip down the side that, especially on the males, becomes much brighter and pronounced during the spawning period and then a shimmering silvery belly. There are dark spots along the length of its body that seem to blend the artistry of this fish into truly a rainbow of colors.

Where the Rainbow Trout lives closer to the coast, originally the Pacific watershed but now also the Atlantic, it will often migrate to the salty water of the ocean after it reaches two years of age. When that urge to spawn again ignites an inner flame, it will return to the cool clear fresh water streams to continue the age old struggle to keep its kind alive. When a Rainbow goes to the sea, it will gradually become more uniform in color as it turns a steel blue or silvery in appearance. The colorful pink stripe on its side will fade considerably or even disappear and it will then be known as a Steelhead Trout. If you are looking at a Rainbow Trout that has lived its entire life in a high mountain stream, or a large Steelhead that has traveled from the Atlantic, through the Great Lakes to the swift moving waters of the St. Joseph River in northern Indiana, you are looking at a *Salmo gairdnerii,* a North American native.

It has been only days since I watched the weakening ice on the river start to give way under the sunbeams of the lengthening days of spring. I could hear the groaning as the thick layers reluctantly succumbed to their own weight as the rivers current deteriorated their under sides. The snow in the valley has mostly melted away and the river rises only slightly, but enough to cast a slight muddy hue to the usually clear and pristine waters of the upper Colorado. It seems that Mother nature has picked a particularly challenging time for the Rainbow Trout to spawn. Not only do the fish have to battle with rivals for ideal nesting sights where their offspring might find some haven of protection, but also sometimes impaired vision due to the cloudy water and the increased current, and debris that has been set afloat by the rising water along the miles of river bank upstream. The rainbow is, however, a lover of colder water than some its cousins and although out of water, it perishes quickly, within its own habitat, it is a remarkably hardy individual. Who can question the ways and wonders of the workings of nature. There is much we will never really understand, and that is a good thing, lest the realm of nature lose her mystery and we humans might somehow think of ourselves as, above it all.

There is another very colorful character that makes his presence known, more so in the spring than any other time of year, the Wild Turkey Gobbler. This grand monarch cannot go without mention. The wild turkey is one of the greatest success stories of wildlife management ever told. When the settlers first arrived in the new world, there were so many wild turkeys that it seemed they were surely an inexhaustible supply of table fare. As we have learned since then, there is no such thing as an inexhaustible natural resource. It has been estimated that in the pre-Columbian era, the population of wild turkeys was over ten million. Contrary to what many of us might think, the American natives did not relish the flesh of the wild turkey, however they did make use of many parts of the bird and so often times would eat it more out of respect or opportunity than preference. Personally I like Wild Turkey more than the domestic variety but I must admit that the drumsticks are full of sinew and difficult to bite into.

A wild turkey is all dark meat, even the breast, which makes it my favorite over the domestic fowl.

Since some of the colonists kept a written record of their beginnings in North America and a few of them wrote about the spectacles that they saw in their new home, we know that there were sometimes as many as five thousand turkeys seen at once, in a single flock! That would definitely be something to write home about. With so many turkeys that were not yet wary enough of man, the settlers naturally relied on them for sustenance in an unfamiliar land. As the years passed, hunters would kill many turkeys in a single day for the market. While they were on their roost at night, they were especially vulnerable. On a night with a full moon, hunters would slip under an entire flock of birds that were silhouetted against a moon lit sky and take several with one shot from a scatter gun. The settlement movement progressed and as it did, vast tracts of virgin forests that supported the turkey population, fell prey to the saw mill. Without the protection of management, and the destruction of their habitat, wild turkeys were disappearing from the eastern states by the early 1800s. By the late 1800s, the Midwest was practically devoid of turkeys. By 1920, eighteen states that had been original turkey habitat, had no wild turkeys at all. It seemed as though the voice of an American spirit would fade away forever and it probably would have without the foresight and dedication of some people to keep this uniquely American symbol alive. In the 1940s, wildlife departments started capturing wild turkeys with nets and relocating them where there was good habitat. By the early 1960s, western states were doing the same for the Rio Grand and Merriam turkeys. In 1986, The population of wild turkeys over the nation had grown to an estimated two million! The only states that did not have a turkey hunting season were Alaska, Nevada and Delaware. The only way this success story was made possible was by the selfless efforts and funding of dedicated sportsmen and women through individual acts and organizations .The wild turkey is native only in America and is truly a grand and magnificent creature

Many times, in the latter half of the green grass moon, has the stillness of the predawn morning found me sitting comfortably against a tree in the woods. The conscious part of me that keeps track of time and activities gives way to a deeper sense of awareness. I feel the coolness of the still morning air, I can smell the freshness of the new spring growth and hear the subtle sounds of the night life going into hiding and the day dwellers beginning to emerge. It seems as though I am part of what is always there, part of the energy that flows through all things when suddenly my attention becomes more focused. I have heard the faint calling of a hen turkey, her waking clucks and tree yelps that seem to trickle down from the tree tops with a liquid quality that is hers alone. The other hens that have shared her resting place begin to join in as the first rays of light appear in the eastern sky and the gobblers that have roosted several yards away, answer with excited gobbles. This is what I came to witness, my attention is riveted to the turkeys. Suddenly there is the flurry of beating wings as the hens fly down from their roost. This excites the gobblers even more and the hens gather around, beneath the gobblers tree in plain view of their suitors. The yelps and clucks of the hens become more intense until finally the gobblers fly down to meet them, this is when the show begins. The gobblers all go into full strut, trying their best to out do one another and attract the attention of the hens. They fluff their feathers until they appear to be twice their actual size, with their heads tucked tightly against their breast they fan their tail and drag their wings and strut in an elaborate display of masculinity. The top of their heads are capped snowy white and the wattles that hang below the beak are swollen and bright red. The broadly fanned tail is an intricate design of brown and black with a black stripe across the top. If these are Merriam turkeys, the tail is tipped with white. As they continue to try to impress their lady friends, they pirouette around in circles. The rising sun will catch the iridescent qualities of their body plumage and reflect blues, greens and yellows from their usually black body. This is a display of nature that is impossible to put into words but can only be truly appreciated through your own eyes.

To really appreciate nature, to grasp the entirety of it you must first let go of what distracts you from it, particularly time and schedules. Try to let go, sometimes, of the logical side and let your senses go to work, allow you instincts to come alive and by all means, look at all the colors.

MAY

⌘

May, the fifth month, according to our present day calendar. As the full moon approaches, the eastern woodland Indians would call it the planting moon, the plains Indians, the moon of green leaves, a time of anticipation and hope for a good growing season and ample provisions for the next winter. To me, May has always seemed like a month of miracles, most of the wildlife community has given birth to another generation of their own kind, the beginning of another cycle, assurance that they remain in the circle of life and will contribute to all who share their path.

These newcomers to the natural world have only a brief time to master the ways of survival that are unique to their kind, ways that have been passed down for the eons that they have inhabited this earth. The dangers that lay before them are many. Some are learning how to stalk and hunt, how to conceal themselves from their prey, while others are learning to watch their surroundings, to test the breeze for the scent of danger and to avoid becoming the meal that the other so desperately seeks. There are triumphs and tragedies that take place every day in the realm of nature. As humans, we try not to think of the agonies and struggles that exist there, but its all part of the great circle. When we take up the role of predator, we need to keep some of that compassion and understanding lest we lose track of our inherent role in the natural and healthy balance we need to help maintain.

There are other new lives coming into being that don't seem to have as many pitfalls to avoid as our other friends that move around. May is a time when the plant community seems to thrive. All the new plants by now, have a good start and seem to be well established. After sprouting from a seed that had fallen in a suitable spot months ago, before the winter winds had blown in a blanket of snow, they continue their annual cycle that has been perpetual since the very beginnings of life on this amazing planet. In my wanderings, I do not go hungry with the bounty of spring all around me. This is when Mother Nature serves up her very best in a banquet that spreads across the land. All of the new young and tender sprouts are at their very best. Many of the tasty edible wild plants are good to eat only at this stage which makes the month of the planting moon also a time of harvest since these tasty morsels can't be stored for any length of time in their fresh state. All of the above ground portions of edible plants are edible now, so the variety of foods available is greatest in the spring. This will change as the plants quickly grow and reach maturity in the short time they are afforded to propagate their seed and guarantee sustenance for the many.

One of our plant friends that makes excellent table fare for just a brief time in the spring is the stinging nettle. There are many of you that would probably consider the stinging nettle something other than a friend, but perhaps if you knew it better you would change your mind. The young shoots of the stinging nettle aren't as likely to sting as when they are older but there is still the need for caution when gathering them, gloves are a very wise choice. Just a few minutes of boiling removes the irritant from the leaves and there is no need to change the water. They can be used as a pot herb, soup, or as a tea and the flavor is good enough to please even the most finicky palate. Nettles are rich in protein, iron and vitamins A and C which makes them better for the body than most garden vegetables and certainly any canned or processed foods. When young, nettles can be gathered with stalk and leaves together since the whole plant is tender and this makes it easy to collect a sizable amount fairly quickly. As the plant grows closer to maturity, you can still gather the new emerging leaves at the tip of the stalk but it is much more time consuming and your more likely to suffer the stinging of the older leaves. The nettles usefulness does not end as it matures, the stalk contains very strong fibers that can be made into a strong and versatile cord, especially in the fall after the plant has dried up and lost its ability to administer pain.

Another good friend that has a short span of edibility is the fireweed. Fireweed gets its name because it is one of the first plants to appear after a forest fire so it can be found in open disturbed areas but is not restricted to such habitat. I have gone to a well established patch of fireweed for a few years now that is hidden in a small ravine and surrounded by lush growth. Eventually natural precession will take over and a different group of plants will take over but there will always be plenty of fireweed for me to find. The small, delicate stalks of fireweed are good either raw or cooked the same way you would asparagus. They have been enjoyed for centuries among different kinds of people. The French trappers that traveled the Mississippi and the Missouri rivers almost two centuries ago referred to fireweed as asparagus and consumed it whenever it was young and tender. When you pluck a new stalk from the ground, it has little leaf scales toward the bottom which makes it look very much like the stalk of an asparagus plant. As it matures, the leaves can be made into tea and have often been used as a substitute for black tea. Fireweed is another good source of fiber that makes a very strong cord.

One of my favorites in the spring is sweet root, also called sweet cicily. There are several varieties of this plant and they vary in their palatability and medicinal strengths. The variety that grows here in the Rockies, *Osmorrhiza chilensis* has a milder flavor than some of its counterparts. Most often it is used to flavor soups, stews and teas, especially teas that have a bitter or overwhelming flavor. In the month of the planting moon, the roots are small and tender as the stalks are indiscreetly appearing among the other foliage, quite often in groves of aspen where the soil is rich and moist. I enjoy them quite often as a raw trail snack. Sweet root is also very good when steamed with other plants or in a stir fry or sliced into a salad of other greens. They have a texture much like that of water chestnuts and add a lively and pleasing taste to your salad of wild plants. Eating sweet root can also be good medicine since it inhibits the reproduction of fungal growth in the body which makes it useful in the treatment of candidiasis. It is also the belief among those that practice natural medicine that it stimulates the mucous membranes of the intestinal tract and aids the body with digestion.

Another treasured delicacy that comes along only in the spring are certain kinds of mushrooms. By the end of this month, in the lower elevations and the Midwest, the season for the morel mushrooms should be done. The morels don't need much introduction since they are such a popular and sought after delicacy. For anyone that has never found them in the spring woods or had the pleasure of tasting them, there is a part of life they haven't experienced yet, and they should. Finding morels in the spring always had my undivided attention each and every year as I was growing up. Mom had no reservations at all about fixing up a scrumptious mess of mushrooms of which not a single crumb would make it to the dish water. Several years ago, when I moved back to the homeland of my wife, the Rocky Mountains of Colorado, I thought there had to be some kind of good mushroom growing in the springtime in the Rockies. Hunting spring mushrooms was an indescribable urge of mine that would not go away. Sure enough, I found something to satisfy my restless spirit, *Discina Perlata,* a member of the peziza group of mushrooms or cup fungi, commonly known as Pigs ears and they quickly became my wife's` favorite. Also growing at the same time was *Gyromitra Gigas* belonging to the gyromitra group or the false morels going by the common name of snow morel. The pigs ears are small and close to the ground with what little stalk there is growing mostly under the soil but they grow in clusters so you always find several in one spot. They also seem to be quite prolific so filling a bag with mushrooms comes easy. Since they are a dense textured fungi, it doesn't take long to gather several pounds of this delicious spring treat. The snow morels however are a different story, we have found them from the size of a golf ball to as large as a football. It is my opinion that the snow morels are every bit as good as the true morels I collected as a boy. The great thing about them is they are much more plentiful than the true morels. I am constantly amazed that few people, it seems, know about these spring delicacies that adorn the mountainsides every spring.

Things are a little different here in the high country than they are down lower, our spring mushrooms usually don't start growing until almost the end of May and will continue well into June. They will first appear, at least here around Hot Sulphur Springs, around eight thousand feet and as the season progresses, we just keep going higher and finding them, usually not far from the snow melt. The snow morels seem to grow quite close to the melt line, in fact, we have found them even growing in the edge of the snow melt.

I guess its pretty obvious where they got their name.

Gathering plants or mushrooms in the spring is not as remotely different from harvesting a deer or elk in the fall as many might think. Both are the act of a life given of one to give life to another. Picking a plant may not seem to carry as much weight as taking an animals life but its a life just the same and deserves the same respect and admiration as any other life. Plants are easier for us to have a negative impact on because they can't avoid us so we need to have a caretaker attitude and be good stewards of our home, enough has been lost already. Mother Earth provides us with much good medicine for the body and for the soul. She deserves good medicine in return. Before you think of what you can take, think about what you can give.

May   Part 2
Places dreams are made of

⌘

The planting moon, a new beginning for another year. May seems more like a beginning than nearly the middle of the year doesn't it? All the new growth, seedlings and the young animals learning the necessities of life. In the circle of the seasons, the planting moon is the start of another cycle, a repeat of the cycles that have been ongoing since life as we know it began on this fragile, watery, celestial ball that is our home. What would it have been like in years past around the abode of the American natives? The people that realized their connection to the earth mother because they relied so directly upon her. One of the most important activities of course was that of planting the seeds that would sprout and grow much of the sustenance for the leaner times that always lay ahead. There would be much thanksgiving for life itself and many prayers and hope that the great spirit would nourish the land and cause their crops to grow. The Grandfather spirit has also caused the bounty of young and succulent plants to feed his people while waiting on the fruits of their labor. The medicine man or woman is very busy collecting the herbs that are so important to the tribe for healing and treating the maladies that affect nearly everyone at one time or another. There is an urgency to gather certain ones before they bloom since they lose their potency while blooming. They concentrate their energy in the act of producing the colors and fragrance of the flower upon which the existence of their kind depends. The medicine man, or medicine woman was truly a caretaker, a steward to the land that sheltered ,fed, and healed their people. They did not ruthlessly or haphazardly tear the plants from the soil. They were grateful for the gift and treated each one with respect. They would take only the ones that were at the proper stage to suit their needs and only enough so as to improve the habitat for those that were left. In this way they were giving back to the earth as well as taking, they were the earth's gardeners.

The cycles that take place through the circle of seasons are many and of great variety. They add diversity and mystery to the ways of the wild. One of our friends in the plant community that caries on a variety of cycles within itself is the Juniper. The Juniper is regarded as a tree, but in the case of the common Juniper, it is more like a bush or a low growing shrub. There are several different species of Juniper that grow in America and they all share some common characteristics. The variety of cycles I mentioned are in the way they propagate their seed. The female cones of this evergreen are born at the leaf axis where the leaf joins the branch while the solitary male cones are at the tip of the branch. The leaves are small and sharp and are usually called needles, like the needles of a pine tree. The little dark blue female cones which are most often in clusters are referred to as Juniper berries. Each year, at the beginning of another growing season, the shrub will produce a crop of new berries while at the same time, waiting on the berries of the last two years to ripen. It can easily take up to three years for a Juniper berry to become fully ripe and fall to the ground. The Juniper has long been looked upon by the eyes of man as good medicine, in some ways reputable and sometimes not. In the Middle Ages, the smoke of a burning Juniper was believed to guard people against the suffering of leprosy and to keep the fairies from replacing their newborn baby with a changeling. The American Indians would brew the branches to relieve a sour stomach and prevent the onset of a cold. The strong, aromatic flavor of the berries make the identification of the Juniper an easy mark and has gained it favor among gourmet chefs. This tiny berry has found its way into stuffing, stews and particularly in the flavoring of wild game dishes. Juniper is also the main ingredient in the flavoring of gin. Juniper has been used medicinally in the Americas since the seventeenth century for relieving gas, to expel worms, cure scurvy and to aid in childbirth. Today's herbal practitioners may use the berries of this spiny shrub as a urinary antiseptic, a carminative and a diuretic. There is some evidence from modern studies that Juniper may be helpful to diabetics who are insulin dependent. If you choose to become better acquainted with this member of the plant community, please remember, there are others that are also close friends with the Juniper. The wildlife that sometimes find nourishment and add variety to their diet with the little blue berries of the Juniper are dependent on what they can glean from the forest. In a healthy population of any wild edible there is enough to share, as long as we make sure that's what we do.

Watching the seasons pass is fascinating as they progress and blend together in the changing from one to another. All over North America, there are similar events that take place as the seasons move along. The variety of habitat and the nuances of the cycles that take place in each and every place have an individual style that gives each different habitat its own personality and beauty and reasons to love it. It can be easy to take some things for granted, and by doing so we miss a great deal of what makes where we live so special.

We can think of many far away and exotic places in the world. What is it that makes those places seem so exotic and wonderful ? What is it that makes them the kind of places we dream about ? Maybe its the landscape, the desert or the mountains, or maybe the lush, deep forests and the wide meandering rivers. It might be the clear rushing streams, or the diverse flora and fauna that grows there. Some of us are intrigued by the spectacular wildlife that lives only there and we dream of being able to go there some day to experience it all. I have not traveled the world or sailed the seas. In a life of nearly half a century, I have seen but just a few little portions of the North American continent yet I have seen the kinds of places dreams are made of. In the Midwest, I have sat among the thick green foliage and listened to the whisper of old man river as he moved and watered and fed the land. I could also feel his sadness for the abuse he carried with him and the disrespect that scarred his banks. There was a short time, many years ago that I spent with the quiet spirit of the desert of the southwest United States. The days were not to harsh at that time, it was in the cooler part of the year. The landscape can seem bleak at first but as I wandered about, the signs of life and sustenance began to appear. I noticed the ever changing features that would take place as the wind would shift the sand, nothing you would notice from a distance but just the covering and uncovering of the little features on the face of the desert floor. As the sun would begin to set, the colors were not just in the western sky but all around. The desert seemed to absorb the fire from the sky and spread it in a splash of colors all around me. When darkness finally overtook the day, the nightlife seemed to ooze from the sand and there was activity all around. I realized, I was not on the desert or at the desert or in any way above it but I was truly in it, immersed in the whole of it and the same as all the rest of it.

After my brief visit with the desert, I traveled west and then north staying inland from the Pacific ocean most of the time. It was all new and wondrous to me since I had never seen the ocean or the many different kinds of habitat that bordered it. Eventually, I found myself camping in the great Redwoods of California. To the folks that see these silent giants every day, I suppose they become accustomed to them as they are a common, everyday sight. To me however, their massive trunks, towering toward the sky made an impression that I will never forget. Looking up, I found myself in the depths of a forest so ancient I could not help but wonder what all they had seen and the caretakers of old that had been their friends. I had never before felt so small and insignificant, a speck among these mighty, age old giants yet at the same time I could sense the life force that bound us together.

After more travels to the north, and then east again, I settled in to a place that I had dreamed of since my very beginnings, the Rocky Mountains. A persons spirit is not confined to space or time and I believe it will lead you home if you can hear its voice in your heart. It was like I had always known this was where I would finally dwell. I had not seen the world, or for that matter, not a lot of the country I lived in, but in my minds eye I had seen many worlds full of things difficult to put into words. I had seen exotic places, the likes of which I never knew before, the kinds of places that definitely, dreams are made of.

As stewards of this great land we have made many mistakes, we have learned from a lot of them and should have heeded many warnings that we haven't. The sooner we learn, the better. We cannot control the whole of our domain. We cannot live separate from nature nor can we live off of the land but rather we must learn again to live with it, to respect it, admire it, love it and care for it. There is no other place on earth like the place we live in, no matter where on earth that might be. Everywhere is wondrous, exotic and exciting and there are dreams there. Listen to your heart, a spirit lives there and knows the path to follow.

JUNE

⌘

June, the sixth month, the middle of the year according to the way modern man tracks the passing of the seasons. It makes no difference what the ancestral origin of each one of us may be, if we were to track our heritage back far enough we would find our forefathers sharing a close relationship with nature. The different times of the year were commonly associated with what was taking place in the realm of nature. The name for the month of June could have been derived from a Latin word that translated into English as *juniores* which meant "youths" or young on the ground. That would seem fitting by observing the wildlife community and all the babies that are being nurtured by their mothers at this time. To the American natives, it would depend on where they lived in America as to what they called this particular part of the cycle of the seasons. To the Cherokee people that lived in a climate that was suitable for farming, this would be DEHALUYI, the green corn moon. The season would be different if you lived among the Cree people that made their homes in the northern great plains. The coolness of spring would linger a little longer there and conditions for growing crops were not as suitable so in their tongue this month would be called SAGIPUKAWIPIZUN or, the moon when leaves come out.

As we peer through the wonders of the workings of nature we see so much diversity, a myriad of life's cycles taking place all the time, each in it's own rhythm, making it's own contribution to all other life on this marvelous planet. For some, an entire life span may be only a matter of minutes or a few hours as with certain insects or microorganisms. There are those in the plant world that sprout from a seed in the spring and die back to the ground in the fall, a period of just a few moons to start life, grow, mature, propagate their own kind and then die. In the animal kingdom, the cycles of life are as varied as the different kinds that belong to it. It seems there is always a cycle of some kind beginning while another is coming to an end, all happening in the midst of another and each one dependent on all the others in order to sustain life as we know it.

With the coming of the summer solstice, which arrives on the twenty first day of the Green Corn Moon, we reach the height of a cycle in the life of the Earth that affects our lives two times a year, the summer solstice marks the longest day of the year. It is not noticeable at first, but now our periods of daylight begin to diminish and will continue to do so until we reach the winter solstice and the shortest day of the year here in the northern hemisphere. These times mark periods in a cycle of one year, or a single trip on our path around the sun. So many things can take place in the course of a year yet in the life of the Earth it has been an instant. Try to imagine how many important and integral cycles take place in all the lives and seasons that make this home of ours what it is during a year, or a century or even during the completion of just one cycle of lunisolar precession that takes twenty six thousand years to complete.

Here in the Rocky Mountains, the Arapaho people called this time "the moon when the hot weather begins" which can be quite true. On a clear day, there is little to shield you from the rays of the sun. The air is dry and lacks the humidity of lower elevations and you can feel the power of the sun the instant that it peeks above the horizon. With the lack of humidity however, it is usually not unbearable to wear a light, long sleeved shirt during the day. Your skin grows tender through the winter months of being protected from the elements so when you first expose it to the sun you are vulnerable to being burned. It only takes a very short while of enjoying the warmth to realize some time later that you are sunburned. Here in the mountains, the sun presents a danger the year around and can cause you much misery if you don't protect yourself.

If we were living in the days of the past, when all of our needs were met by the gracious Mother Earth, the green corn moon would bring us a sense of security and assuredness that many good days lay ahead. There are all the new, fresh greens and salad plants growing that we can enjoy only at this time of year. The weather is warm and the nights enjoyable and living is again easy but we are not without things that need to be done. The steps of preparation that are necessary for survival never cease but at least our conditions of living become much better during the warm months. The medicine man or woman's gathering of plants and herbs will not end until the winter has spread it's covering over the land. The gathering of medicine that is so important to the needs of the people is a diverse and complicated art. Some plants have much to offer when they are young while others hold their powers in their roots or blooms. Many times they take on different characteristics as they grow and some are best in their first or second season of life. It all depends on what plant you are seeking and what you are asking of it. Perhaps you are in need of a topical remedy for a sprained muscle, a swollen joint or stiff muscles. Heart leaf Arnica will gladly supply you with a poultice or tincture that will relieve you of your pain, provided you are thankful for the gift. You must however, procure a specific part of this plant brother at the proper time. Arnica holds it's power in the root and in the showy, pretty yellow flower which will appear from May to July, depending on the immediate climate and habitat. Here in the Middle Park region of the Rocky Mountains of Colorado, my friend Arnica usually starts to bloom well into June in the River valleys and in July as you reach higher elevations. The root can sometimes be a little difficult to obtain. Although the roots are rhizomes that grow horizontally beneath the soil surface, they work their way under and around rocks and other roots of Pine trees and neighboring plants. Although the root is a very powerful part of the plant, the taking of the root will end the life of that particular plant. Arnica won't develop a flower until its second year of growth so by taking the root in the early part of the year, you could be destroying an immature plant that hasn't yet gained the power of an older plant. A life will be gone and your medicine is not as strong as it could have been had you taken more care in collecting and taken a moment to communicate with your plant brother, he might have let you know the error of your ways. Once Arnica starts blooming, it will do so every year there after as long as it lives. When you take on the attitude of thanksgiving and humility of a true caretaker of the earth, you will pay close attention to the population densities of the plant friends that fill your needs. Then you can help your plant brothers by thinning them where they grow close together and leaving them alone where they do not need any care and by so doing improve on their habitat and they will be better off because of you. That is the part where you do the giving instead of the taking.

I have used Arnica as an example but the gardener attitude is not restricted to one plant or a group of plants or even the plant community for that matter. Whether the Earth Mother has provided you with medicine or food, plant or animal, it should be regarded as a gift, Mother Nature owes nothing to anyone. In this day of trophy hunting and gathering herbs for money, there is much taking and not nearly enough giving. There is nothing wrong with testing your wits and savvy in the pursuit of a certain animal or certain kind of animal, and there is nothing wrong with gathering herbs for your personal use or to help a friend, as long as it is done with the right frame of mind and a genuine sense of gratitude that comes from the heart. When the Grandfather saw all that he had made, he knew that it was good, not just good for the people alone, but good for all things on the face of the Earth. With taking, something comes to an end. With giving, there is no end.

June Part 2
It is all one

As I survey my surroundings I see many things, some are comforting and uplifting, good for the soul. I am never alone but continually surrounded by friends. I am cared for, my discomforts and maladies healed and my body fed. No matter where I look I see my plant brothers and sisters, all my four legged friends that roam the wilds, the free spirits that soar across the sky and the wet ones that rest in the shade at the edge of the lakes and streams. Truly I am surrounded by the vitality of life, the singing of the birds and the breath of Mother Earth as she whispers in the trees and the water that falls from father sky to nourish the land. There is no separation from one to another, one can not exist without the presence of the other, it is all one.

Behind my lodge, to the north across the river, there is a mountain called Mt. Bross. This mountain is not a big mountain, not by comparison with some others that I can see further away along the continental divide. Mt. Bross doesn't reach above the timberline nor is it one of those inspiring lofty peaks that you see on a postcard or in a painting. This mountain does however, protect my abode from some of the strong north winds in the winter. When I find myself on top, I am provided with some spectacular scenery and a view of many miles in all directions. Mt. Bross is much more than a windbreak, or an excellent vantage point, it is more than just a mountain with someone's name, it is home to many of my beloved friends that I have been blessed with the opportunity to meet over the years. One is the great Bald Eagle that upon occasion I will see coursing just above the tree tops following the curves of the river in search of a trout, or resting on the rock face while greeting the morning sun on the easterly face of the mountain. There is also the big tom Cougar that one time surprised my oldest son Adam by seemingly appearing out of nowhere and watching him from the rocks above where my son was resting. Adam, not being prone to flee and wise to the ways of the wild enjoyed the visit from one of the four legged ones and accepted his confrontation with the cat as just that, a visit. There is a place on the north side of Mt. Bross that the Elk like to use during the rutting season. It is surrounded by fairly heavy timber and is a flat and comfortable place for lazing about in the midday and for the bulls to do their courting. Almost all of the north side is so steep that in climbing it I become, for a short time, one of four legged ones. That flat area, about one hundred yards or so in diameter is a favorite place of the Elk. Once, while I was in that spot in mid summer, leaning against an old pine tree enjoying the coolness of the thick woods, three bull Elk came feeding their way towards me. Having the tree to shield me from their view, they approached within a few feet from where I stood. I could see their nostrils flaring as they tried to pick up a scent that would inform them of what that unfamiliar lump was on the side of the tree. I could smell their pungent aroma and hear the guttural sounds coming from their stomachs as they digested the lush mountain grass they had been grazing on. I could see their eyes as they rolled to take in their surroundings and keep themselves constantly aware of everything around them. The lead bull took quite some time studying that eyeball stuck to the side of that old pine tree before he finally decided he would rather walk back down the mountain than past that unusual sight. I have been on all sides of this mountain and have visited all of it's secret places and the stories of those I have met could go on and on but this is not about me or my experiences other than to personify Mt. Bross. Compared to the region that surrounds this mountain, it is but a little piece of everything around it, yet the importance of it to those that live there is unparalleled and the different habitats that exist there make it the kind of special place it is.

The American Natives were confused by the concept of land ownership. It was hard for them to understand how a person could own a rock, or a section of river or how one area of land could be separated from the rest, after all, was not all the land one? How could you posses the water in a stream when it was constantly changing? The water that is yours now was not where it is just a little while ago nor will it be the same in the next moment. That would be like capturing the wind and keeping it for yourself. In this day and age there has to be some standards and even ownership to maintain some kind of order in the ever increasing invasion of mankind. There are circumstances that provide some with the ability to gain more than what seems to be their fair share which can create an evil thing in the minds of men, greed. Greed is what causes one to look at things only in monetary value instead of it's true worth, like the land.

Development of land into residential areas is taking place at an alarming rate. When we have sapped the land for all it's worth, have padded our bank account, bought fancy cars and built luxurious homes, where will our fresh air come from? What will we do to keep our water, the key to life as we know it, clean and healthy? What about all those that called these places home before they were driven elsewhere? These very things have been taking place for quite some time now. Our air and water is already threatened. After building roads further into wild places and taking up residence, people have more and more incidents with wild animals and all to often, the animal gets portrayed as the bad guy. I don't believe that these things happen, for the most part, because people have bad or unreasonably selfish intentions at heart. They happen simply by not knowing the results of their actions or never being made aware of the importance of stewardship of the little piece of land they have been allowed to claim ownership of. All of us being to some extent, a product of our environment, should be allowed to enjoy the finer things in life, to be able to gain some rewards for our diligence and hard work. If we are fortunate enough to live in a beautiful and uncrowded place then we need to learn how to coexist with those that were there before us, to respect them, and by so doing, enjoy their company and let them be who they are.

In northern Indiana there is a special place, a place where the different tribes of people that lived around the southern shore of Lake Michigan and the surrounding vicinity would gather. They would build their council fires and talk about the matters of the people without any prejudice or ill feelings for this was a place that the Great Spirit had given them for camaraderie and understanding and peace. This place is now the Indiana Dunes State Park. Many people visit the Dunes each year to camp, hike, swim in the southern most of the Great Lakes and learn about the habitat at the nature center. It seems the Great Spirit has truly blessed this place, even for modern man, when you see how friendly people can be to strangers that for a weekend have become their neighbors. The people that are in charge of maintaining this special place do a remarkable job of keeping it clean and protecting the habitat for all to enjoy but there are hazards that sometimes befall a place regardless of the efforts made to protect it. There are dangers that lurk in this place on the southern shore of Lake Michigan and not only does it affect the delicate habitat that has thrived there for centuries, but also the people that go there to enjoy it. What could cause such a thing ? You guessed it, land development. There is an intricate system of wetlands that drain into Lake Michigan from the park and from areas south of it. These marshes and wetlands with their dense foliage and root systems, the settling areas and meandering water courses have always been the filtering system of the water running into the lake. Outside the park, where the stewards of the land have no control, land development has destroyed parts of these wet lands and the effect of the filtering system has been depleted to the extent that harmful bacteria sometimes reach the waters of the Great Lake. In times of heavy rain or extra runoff, the public beach has to be closed to swimmers because of the presence of things that shouldn't be there. Here again, the land has been dealt a blow without even considering the ramifications, the delicate habitat and those that live there and also those that visit.

In all our years of culture, education and scientific discoveries, it is sad that there are some that can be so easily blinded by excessive wealth. I can not understand how the matters of the land and it's importance to our future is not common knowledge. Maybe it is that some just refuse to see it. No matter how many boundaries we put up or how many parcels we divide the land into, the land will not recognize it, it can't recognize it because to the land there is no division or separation of one part from another, there simply are no parts, it is one. However we decide to conjure up property lines and boundaries we need to remember that the whole land functions as one and we can not cut the arteries of Mother Earth or obstruct the flow of life in one part of her without upsetting a balance that is as important to us as it is to all other life as well. From the whole Earth, comes all life.

July

⌘

July, another label on yet another period of time, the seventh month of the year. Another period in the continuing circle of the seasons that has been given a name and a number. A name that has been changed periodically through the ages. The big difference between the minds of men and the workings of nature is that sometimes people seem to make changes in an abrupt and sometimes frivolous manner where nature is quite often slow and deliberate. The changes that take place in the realm of nature are subtle and constant and go very much unnoticed, but have shaped the face of our planet and the life that lives on it into the wonderful and mysterious place that it is.

July, in the days of the early Romans was called Quintilis which represented the fifth month. After the adoption of the Julian calendar it was renamed, "Julius" in honor of Julius Caesar. In middle and early modern English, the name Julius was written July, thus the name of the month that we use to this day. The

Lakota people of the American west called this month the "moon of the red cherries" or 'canpa< 'sa wi. Here again, this was from an observation of what was taking place in the natural world around them as they saw it. A way of describing the things to come, to stay mindful of the preparation for the needs of life that continue through the ever changing circle of the seasons, for the next moon will be the moon of ripening.

July is one of the warmest months of the year in North America. Many people suffer each year from heat exhaustion and dehydration because of the heat, and many times because they went unprepared. In this modern age, we are used to having everything we need close by or at our finger tips so it's easy to lose some of that survival mentality. Proper clothing and water are necessities any time of the year.

As always, the people that lived close to the earth were in a constant state of preparation. People all over the world, people of all races and cultures have at some time lived close to the earth. They relied entirely on the gifts from the Earth Mother to nourish them, heal them and give them shelter. They took nothing for granted and held a sense of gratitude and respect for all things. They could not consider their life as harsh or unfair, there were no other options. They lived and breathed like all other things they shared life with and considered themselves no more and no less a part of nature than anything else. Man however, has in the course of time, realized some of his advantages. He has the mental and physical ability to change his surroundings and habitat in order to improve his way of life. Mankind has been endowed with the power of imagination and creativity. He has been blessed with a sense of humor and spirituality and also the ability to make comparisons and to learn from his mistakes, to provide a more comfortable future for those yet to come. Without these abilities, mankind in his frailty, probably would have never flourished.

The people of the past realized their dependence on nature. The changes they made in their surroundings did not go on without strong consideration of the impact they were making on those they shared their life with. Their actions were never meant in any way to master or conquer a place, but to improve upon it, not only for their own lives but also for all others that lived there. Most often, the natives of America, could see no way that they could improve upon the intricate workings of nature. There were however, occasions when they learned to blend the elements without creating a negative effect on their surroundings.

There were people that lived in the desert southwest of North America as long as 2000 years ago that improved their way of living in the dry, arid and inhospitable region of the Sonoran Desert. The Hohokam people who were the ancestors of the Paiute, learned how to manage their most precious resource, water. They built a canal system that extended over many miles through varied terrain that connected to a distant river and provided water to the parched and dry environment of the desert. They did not just simply dig ditches but understood the effects of evaporation. It would have been much easier to dig wider, shallow canals but instead, they knew the need to dig them deep and narrow. A design intended to carry an adequate volume and to lessen the amount of surface water that would be subject to evaporation. By doing this, they not only met their own need for water but also created a long and winding oasis through the parched desert landscape. This man made oasis eventually gave way to greater populations of animal life and plant life that flourished in a once dry land. This also provided the people with meat and vegetable food to add to the crops they could now plant and harvest. The Hohokam people had certainly improved on their way of life and also on the lives of those around them. The future of the people had been strengthened as was their bond to the Earth Mother, and their kinship with all other life had been made stronger.

Since the time of the Hohokam people and their ancient lifestyle, there have been many changes made by the hand of man that has affected the landscape, the environment and the habitat of many places on this fragile, tiny, watery sphere we call home. When it comes to the construction of huge dams and power plants, mining prospects for fossil fuel in remote areas and urban development in pristine settings, how much thought was given to Mother Nature? How much consideration went toward our furred and feathered brothers and sisters that live there?

Not far from my home there is a railroad that carries miles of train cars full of coal each day. At times I have watched them pass and I am amazed, awe struck at the amount of coal that lumbers past and then I am saddened when I picture in my mind the enormous scar left on the face of the Earth Mother from where all this fuel was taken. I have to wonder, is it taken and used with gratitude? Do we thank the Creator each day for our lights and heat in our homes? How much consideration was given to the habitat and what has been given back for what has been received? I, like you, enjoy the comforts provided by modern living, our easy access to energy and transportation. I also realize that these things are necessary for our way of life to continue but do you ever wonder, how much is enough and how long can it possibly last?

There are many groups of honorable people out there that belong to sponsored organizations and also state and governmental agencies that try to promote conservative measures when it comes to our diminishing and irreplaceable natural resources. I know, many of these people don't enjoy a high level of popularity but, if it weren't for these people, all would soon be lost to enterprise and capitalism, the all mighty buck. There has, during the last century, been a heightened awareness among the human race of our dependence on the Earth and visa versa, but it seems the rekindling of our relationship with the Earth and the recognition of our responsibility as caretakers as a whole, remains in the distance.

Recently, my wife Maryann, and the boys and I drove from Colorado to the Gulf of Mexico and stayed on Padre Island for a few days. As always, I was enthralled with the changes that took place as we traveled from the cool high mountains of Colorado, through the warm, humid landscape of Texas and on to the sultry breezes that drifted inland from the Gulf coast. I noticed the changing horizons, the way the stars seemed to go all the way to the ground and surround me in the night sky. As I peered into space, I again realized just how tiny and insignificant I was compared to the myriad of life around me and the expanse of space that was spread out before me. While traveling during the day, I saw the habitat and scenery change, the different kinds of wildlife, the changing plant communities, the difference in the color of the water in the lakes and rivers. When we stopped I couldn't help but take in the soil that I was not accustomed to and the insect life and birds and snakes that I had never met. As we neared the coast, the predominant breezes from the west gradually shifted until the faint and mellow scent of salt air greeted us from the east. Finally we were moving across the shallow salt flats between the island and the mainland. Just inhaling the breath of the ocean seemed to awaken some ancient spirit hiding within me. In a short while, we were on the gulf side of the island and waded out into the rich, warm waters, unique to anywhere else on Earth. In the water I became oblivious to the human activity around me, the signs of thoughtless people scattered along the beach, and time, it was just the ocean and me. It was another one of those brief, yet eternal moments. I could feel the energy from the countless forms of life around me, flowing through me. The surf washed over my face and the taste of the salt of the Earth was in my mouth. My feet gently brushed along the sand on the bottom while I drifted along with the rhythmic beat from the pulse, the heartbeat of Mother Earth. My physical boundaries melted away as I flowed with the current of the ancient circle of life. I felt a deep sense of gratitude as I looked through Father Sky toward the great mystery, and gave thanks. Not for anything in particular in my life, but for life itself, all of it.

To be true caretakers, we need to notice, be aware of the many cycles, lives and entities that makes this world work. There are many things in the matters of nature we do not understand and never will. The secrets and the mysteries that are held in the workings of Mother Nature are vital to our humanity and our humility. By observing the world around us, from the expanses that spread out before us to the spaces between the grains of sand, Nature provides us with much more than sustenance. She gives us gratitude, inspiration and a sense of belonging and sharing. In this day, we are still a part of all things, so what has an effect on the Earth, has an effect on us. When you go out, be it some remote wilderness setting, or your backyard, absorb the energy of life around you, experience the moment and remember, you are a part of all of this. We are all members of the community of life, let us do our best to make it better.

July Part 2
Living waters

Water, the stuff of life. The most abundant chemical compound on Earth. A very simple molecule compared to many others yet it is essential to all living organisms and also plays a major role in the environment in which they live.

A water molecule, H2O, is made up of only three atoms, two hydrogen and one oxygen. They share a mutual bond of a pair of electrons between each hydrogen atom and the oxygen atom that holds them together. The oxygen atom holds a partial double negative electrical charge while each hydrogen atom has a partial positive charge. Although the water molecule holds these positive and negative charges, it is electrically neutral. It does however have a negative pole at the oxygen atom and a positive pole centered between the hydrogen atoms.

When I think about that single little molecule of water, as simple as it may seem, there is so much activity that takes place in such a miniature space and there are continuing cycles that go on there. They are the very cycles of life that go on throughout the universe. The energies that form everything we see, feel, and touch, the unity of all things. To me, a molecule of water is nothing short of a miracle.

Three tiny atoms form one tiny molecule, invisible to the naked eye, seen only with the help of a very powerful microscope. Lump enough of them together and you have a drop of water, enough drops and you have a cup of the refreshing, cleansing, rejuvenating stuff of life.

Water can take on many forms. The liquid form that comes as rain, that we drink, bathe and swim in. The frozen state of water, ice, we cool our drinks with it and it stores much of the earth's water in the polar ice caps and snow. It also allows us to easily travel across bodies of water in the winter. Then there is the gaseous form that is in our atmosphere, in the clouds we see drifting above us, the steam rising from a cup of tea or the hot springs in Yellowstone, the morning fog and what we exhale with every breath.

All of the elements on the earth and its atmosphere never leave, they are contained within our sphere of life. The air we breath and the water we use is the same air and water that has been here since the birth of the planet. They have never been replenished, they never will be, they are recycled by nature. The plants breath in what we and all the other mammals breath out and we breath in what the plants breath out. The earth's hydrosphere is all its water, glacial ice and moisture in atmospheric gases. Water and ice cover nearly three fourths of the entire planet and the oceans make up 98% of the whole hydrosphere. Very much of the earth's water is in a constant state of circulation, another one of those cycles of life called the hydrologic cycle. Every year about 118 quadrillion gallons, or 107,000 cubic miles of water evaporates into the atmosphere and then 90% of it returns to the oceans by different forms of precipitation, rain, hail & snow. The remaining 10% falls on land and creates our fresh water supply in the form of lakes, rivers and ground water which seeps through the ground and collects in underground aquifers. This ground water is by far our most generous supply of fresh water and supplies on the average, 20%

to 50% of the water in all of the rivers and streams. As this water is filtered down through the soil and slowly moved through marsh areas it is recycled naturally, and again made fit for use by us and our furred and feathered friends. As water falls to the earth in the form of precipitation, a single part of the many involved in the cycle of planetary hydration, much more happens than just water falling. The Earth Mother, in the act of living, breathing and perspiring, supplies all things with their need for water. Some of the precipitation evaporates back to the atmosphere before it reaches the ground. Some of it is captured in snow and ice fields where it might stay for a single season or many thousands of years. More of it is caught by the leaves of trees and bushes and the many countless plants that immediately absorb it. The remainder that makes it to the soil becomes the life giving force that again courses through the veins of the good earth.

Water being such an essential ingredient of life, it seems like we, the stewards of the earth, would treat it with utmost care. The value of this gift has been seriously taken for granted.

The Great Lakes lie in east central North America and share the border between Canada and the United States. They are made up of five connecting lakes, Lake Superior, Lake Michigan, Lake Huron, Lake Erie and Lake Ontario. Together the five lakes form the largest body of fresh water in the world. The entire Great Lakes basin which includes the land between the lakes takes up 295,200 square miles. In years past, American Natives of several tribes lived in and around these wondrous and magnificent bodies of water. They had more than enough fresh water to supply their needs, an abundance of game and fish, great stores of plant and vegetable foods and rich soil to grow many crops. They also had copper which they learned to make many utensils, ceremonial items and weapons out of. Extensive travel and trade among the other tribes was made possible by canoeing along the great waterways. The Indians were very grateful for where they lived and the gifts they received from the land and waters that they had the honor to share their lives with. Things have sadly changed in the last couple of centuries.

All of the Great Lakes have suffered greatly from pollution and misuse. They have become a dump sight for everything from toxic chemicals to abandoned ships. Lake Erie, the second smallest and the shallowest of these five huge providers of life has suffered the most. Lake Erie borders four states in the U.S., Michigan, Ohio, New York, Pennsylvania and the Canadian province of Ontario. The shores bordering the lake are home to twelve and a half million people. Many of these people of today are deeply saddened by the effects of years of shortsighted practices of industry and farming. There are many who fight for the good of the lake and the quality of life around it and the other Great Lakes, but reversing the effects takes large fortunes, much time and a long cooperative effort between mankind and Mother Nature. Since the 1960s, when ecologists said the lake would soon become a dead lake, some things have changed in the way of industrial, human waste and farming discharge into the lake. It is helping but there is still a long road ahead.

Rivers are the arteries of life, many of them still carry the names given them by the natives that inhabited their banks. Their courses and canyons, slow meanderings and magnificent waterfalls have instilled wonder and awe, inspiration, spirituality and mystery in the hearts of people from the time of our ancestors to now.

Rivers have carried man on his journeys of trade and discovery, they have made legends of those that have traveled their many miles. The Missouri River carried Louis and Clark and the Corp of Discovery on one of the greatest endeavors of exploration ever taken by a group of people. Rivers have been subject to the same misuse and abuse as the Great Lakes. In my lifetime I have canoed in waters that I could drink and see the fish that nourished my body. I could feel its goodness and wholeness in my body as well as in my soul. I have also floated along rivers that were filled with old clothes washers and dryers, parts of automobiles and refrigerators. The banks were strewn with piles of cans and bottles and all kinds of trash imaginable. I could not help but ask, why here? Why in the river? Who could possibly be so cruel and unappreciative? In places where I grew up, camping, catching fish and being taught by my father to appreciate nature and respect it, to give it the honor it deserves, there are warnings about eating the fish, they are contaminated. How did we ever allow these things to happen to the very things that allow us to live on this beautiful planet? There is some consolation. Efforts have been underway for some time to clean up our waterways. There are some streams that are running cleaner than they have since 1930, but we must not rest on our laurels, there is so much more to do.

For the generations that have lived on this earth, many mistakes have been made and many lessons have been learned. In this modern age it seems we have come so far, made so many discoveries and have learned so much about what makes our world work the way it does. We are however, still making mistakes, we still have so much to learn. We will never fully understand everything about nature. There will always be mysteries we can't unravel, secrets we can't pull from their hiding place. We must never allow ourselves to think we have risen to such a level that nature does not deserve our respect and thanksgiving for all the gifts we receive, whether we understand them or not.

In the grand circle of life, there are many parts that work together to make the whole, we are one of those parts.

AUGUST

⌘

Since ancient times man has observed the many cycles of nature that take place on the Earth and in the worlds around it. We have marveled at the stars and named constellations after those perceived as immortal. For the length of mans recorded history he has watched the skies, pondering and studying the countless celestial bodies that seem to move along the same giant path that we also are on. It has been the endeavor of some people from every generation to find some continuity with our place in the great circle and all of those that follow it, a way to place our history within a frame, a way to accurately record the passing of time.

No matter how far we look into space, or how many comparisons we make between ourselves and the movements of the heavenly bodies, our framework of time has been determined mostly by our nearest neighbor, the moon. The problem with using the lunar phases of the moon, is that the twelve phases of the moon, a lunar year, do not correspond with the length of a solar year.

People from all over the world, from different times and various cultures have established different calendars with their own set of annual celebrations, traditions and holidays. These many various civil calendars have almost always originated with the twelve lunar phases of the moon, along with some variations to try to compensate for the difference in the length of the solar year. According to the Julian calendar, which was reformed from the ten month Roman calendar in 46 B.C., Easter, a spring holiday, would have eventually taken place in the middle of the summer. In 1582 the adoption of the Gregorian calendar, and the incorporation of the leap year which attempted to correct the deviations between lunar and solar years, was accepted by France and the Netherlands. Nearly four hundred years passed before the rest of the world accepted it as it is used today.

Man has always been a restless creature. Due to his physical inadequacies, he is constantly on the move, in search of the necessities of life. He needs to provide food, shelter, and clothing from sources apart from himself. We also need to look after the comfort and welfare of our families and communities. These are things that have not changed since the beginning of mankind and to this day are the essence of our survival. In the course of time our interests and wants have become confused with necessity. Our quest for the needs of life have become so varied, our measuring of time so precise, that ironically, we run out of time. So often I've heard it said that there is not enough time in the day to do all the things that need done. Is it possible that we have found a way to exhaust our only inexhaustible resource? Not at all. If you can't always take time for yourself, you can occasionally make time. Time is relative only to what you do with it. Go out and watch a sunset. As the Earth rolls along its path, we travel with it along its journey. The sun lowers in the sky and the clouds begin to cast their shadows across the land, eastward grows the dimming figures of the trees and hills. Eventually the sun begins to lose its intensity and on the horizon are the reflections of the thin atmospheric veil that protects the earth. The changing hues of color, the mixtures of red and yellow swirl across the sky and reach a brilliance that has never been matched by the stroke of an artist. The dimming light of day gradually gives way to the darkness of the night sky through which it seems you can see for an eternity. The lights of stars that have been gone for ages are still filtering down to us, mysteries incomprehensible to mankind are all following the same giant path of life. This brief moment, this time you allowed yourself to watch the passing of a day, to ponder those things close and far away, was nothing more than a moment, a moment in which time had no meaning, a moment in which you made the time to absorb the beauty around you.

The native Americans also had their way of keeping track of time. They, like other people around the world, followed the phases of the moon. Their lifestyle was simple and was governed more by the cycles of nature and the seasons. To them, the phases of the moon and the signs of the seasons marked what part of the year was on hand or was approaching. It kept them vigilant in their preparation for the coming changes, and aware of how long their current provisions needed to last. They lived a simple life. The land did not belong to them but rather they belonged to the land. They had no desire to try to change or control that which the creator had designed, only to merge with the flow of life, to be as one with all things. By watching the passing of the moon they were kept aware of what was necessary now and what would follow as they carried on with the task of living. By observing all that was around them, they knew how well the Earth Mother had provided for their needs in this moment of the circle of the seasons.

This, the eighth passing of the moon, to the people of the Rocky mountains and the high plains, is the moon of ripening. A busy time of gathering and drying much of the grain, nuts and berries that will carry their tribe through many moons until the return of fresh fruit and vegetable foods. With the coming of the moon of colored leaves, there will be preparation for hunting. There will be praying and dancing and purification to become worthy of accepting the gift of life they will receive from their four legged brothers and sisters. Although on a good year this can be a time of plenty, it can also be a trying time. This time of preparation must be shared with others that are in need of sustenance for the cold months ahead.

When the native Americans of yesteryear would go to gather a winters store of grain and berries, they were often met by Mato-Wakan-Ska, the great Grizzly Bear, also in the act of preparing for a long winter. The great bear, needing a thick layer of fat for hibernation, would enter into a state of gluttony and would welcome a meal of meat, be it animal, human or carrion along with the sweet berries and rich grains of his coming autumns feast. The bear knows no spite or contempt, he holds no malice in his heart. He carries with him the will to live and the instinct for survival, the need to get fat and be warm and nourished for a long winters sleep.

Today, our lives seem a world away from the way life was a couple of centuries ago. Our lives are not dependent on gathering food or preparing for the changing seasons. For most of us, our existence is not threatened by the onset of fall and winter. Many of us it seems have gone from preparation to procrastination. Almost everything we need is at our fingertips, the supermarket or the convenience store. We have lost sight of what lies beyond a measured block of space and time. We get what we need when we need it. This is simply the convenience of modern living. How convenient is it ? We are so busy in the act of living, working, running from here to there to get the things we need, planning schedules, making money, spending money, trying to fit all we can into a time frame that seems to take up every minute of every day. We are all bound by time, we cannot escape it, it will always find us. When we break away from it, it will eventually make its presence known, so it is all right to once in a while, try to escape from it.

Unlike those that live in the realm of nature, our lives are governed so much by the measuring of time. To truly experience nature, we need to enter into a dimension many of us are not accustomed to, a realm not hindered by the measuring of time. For those of us that choose to spend time outdoors, we need to be prepared for an absence from time. It would be irresponsible to abandon our future or our lives and those that share it with us. Our affairs must be in order to comfortably allow ourselves a break from keeping track of time. Once we have prepared ourselves by meeting all of our current obligations, we can enjoy the luxury of just noticing the passing of time. We can watch the beginning of a new day, a day that has never been experienced and never will again. There is pleasure in seeing the miracles of life, a butterfly floating on its wings or a mother deer coaching her young one in the ways of life. It is soothing to the soul to hear the bugling of the majestic bull elk as he gathers his herd, or the bubbling of a mountain stream, the singing of a sparrow, the breeze whispering through the trees. It quiets my spirit to smell the aroma of the earth, and to read with my nostrils the messages carried by the brothers of the four winds. There is comfort in feeling the warm sun on my face, or the coolness of snowflakes gently touching my face and hands. I am at peace while reflecting on the whole day at the end of it with no worry of how long it took to pass.

Many things have changed for me since I was a boy. Time used to be so easy to escape. The workings and wonders of nature, the miracles of life kept my curiosity alive for days that seemed like an eternity. Now I have a family of my own. They need me and I need them. Whether my trips outdoors are alone or shared with my wife and children, my affairs at home must be in order so we can fully enjoy our outdoor experience.

I have become better through years of practice and mistakes at preparing for an outdoor excursion. I have learned how to recognize and accept those gifts that Mother Nature provides for my needs and comfort. With the right frame of mind I can still enjoy the wonders of life in the natural realm. I still have days that go on forever. I understand more than I used to but my curiosity never fades. Each day is a new day, each experience unique to any other and every time away from time is cherished.

I am honored to be able to share with my children and others what the teachers without words have shown me. I am deeply touched when I hear my sons give thanks for a gift of life before they touch it I saw a tear in my youngest sons eye as he offered his gratitude to the great spirit and to the first elk that was given him to help feed his people. I have watched my eldest son, who never had the desire to hunt or fish, gather plant foods from the earth mother with the thanks and reverence due the creators garden.

There are those that call me a teacher yet there is so much I learn from them. We can seek to gain knowledge and understanding but if we listen to those that speak without words, we might be given a little wisdom as well. Time will go on whether we keep track of it or not.

August Part 2
Many Branches

Along the winding path of mankind there are many branches. Not everyone will travel the same way or follow the same lifestyle. Through our journey we have formed many different tribes, many different philosophies and beliefs. Our cultural diversity is a powerful tool that can forge new concepts and reinforce old truths. By living in a society of as many intellectual specialties as we do, the sharing of knowledge should make us better at sharing life.

There are those that are completely satisfied to live their lives within the city and they should not be expected to change their way of life. They are important and valuable contributors to society and make a visible impact on the community. There are also those of us that carry with us that ancestral fire that gives us the need to experience nature, to blend with the basics of life, to feel the movement of the circle of life. The extent to which we experience nature also comes in many different levels. Some of us are skiers, snowboarders and snowmobilers that enjoy the winter season. There are campers, hikers and boaters that venture out during the warmer months. In the fall, the hunters enter into the most basic of the dynamics of life, the simple truth that it takes life to give life. Regardless of how you spend your time outdoors, your enjoyment comes from the gifts of nature, be it snow, food or just solitude and an escape from time. When we treat these gifts with respect and gratitude and responsibility, we make a less visible but no less important impact on the community of life as a whole. I believe that when you go to the home of your wild brothers and sisters with a caring attitude, you will fuel that instinctual ember that glows within you. In time you will feel the connection that holds you to all other life and travel beyond the observers stage and become an active and important participant.

This being the moon of ripening, there is opportunity to gather some of the truly delectable treasures of the earth. Gathering berries and making jams and jellies used to be a common thing. I can remember as if it were yesterday the aroma of wild fruit cooking in my Grandmothers kitchen and her telling me to lick the mixing bowl so that none would go to waste. During this month while there are people camping and hiking and enjoying the outdoors, they often find the most common and well known berry, the wild raspberry. Growing throughout most of America, the sight of this tasty morsel seems to ignite that hunter, gatherer instinct in all of us. Children are especially attracted to the red, slightly fuzzy little berry that stands out among the green foliage of the bush. They can hardly resist the urge to taste it. Parents and guardians should be aware that not all red berries are good to eat. The wild raspberry is easily identified and doesn't look like any of the toxic red berries but sometimes small children, or over zealous adults don't see past the appealing color. One of those toxic red berries to watch for is baneberry, it has been responsible for illness and death in many children. Unlike the raspberry that grows on a bush with many branches, lined with needle sharp barbs, baneberry is an upright, perennial herb that has a single cluster of red or white shiny berries at the tip of a smooth, barbless stalk. There is no need to be afraid of a raspberry, just take the time to positively identify what you pick. The raspberry, being very soft and fragile when it is ripe should be gathered with gentle care. The fleshy part of the berry will slip off of the small inner core with nothing left to remove before you taste the sweetness of this little gift from the earth. If you choose to make jam or jelly from the raspberry, there are many tiny seeds that will separate from the berry while cooking and will settle at the bottom of the pan. These should be removed before canning or the last couple of jars you fill will be mostly seeds.

One of my favorites is the currant berry. Here in the Rocky Mountains we have both red and black currants, the most common being the black variety. The currant bush also has spreading branches with smaller barbs than the raspberry and leaves that closely resemble that of the maple tree but smaller. The berries hang from the bottom side of the branches and may range from the size of a pea to as big as a marble. At first it may seem there are not a lot of berries to be picked but by lifting the branch to look at the underside there are sometimes many of those tasty morsels lined up along the length of the branch. The berries of the currant bush are always round and have the remnants of the bloom still attached to the bottom of the berry, opposite the stem. Although the are many varieties of currants, there are none that will make you ill. While picking currants, the stem will usually stay with the berry and the little dried tuft of the bloom will always be there so the berries will need to be cleaned before cooking. The seeds are so small and few that if you are making jam instead of jelly, there is no need to remove them.

There have been times when there was not enough rain during the summer and the currant bushes struggled to produce very much of their fruit. This is when I abstain from picking berries. To my family and l, the jams and jellies made from natures garden are an occasional treat. To the bears and the birds, they are a necessary part of their survival. There is much pleasure and satisfaction in being able to accept and use the gifts of the earth. There is also the same feelings that come along with being aware of the needs of others and knowing how to share with those that need what you only want.

The chokecherry is a very popular fruit of the western states. Although it grows in many of the plains and northern states, it is sought after in the mountain states because the are no fruit orchards that grow in very dry or high altitude climates. The chokecherry is a small tree that may reach a height of about twelve feet in the western mountains. Most often you will find several of them growing together where mother nature has nurtured from seed an orchard of her own kind to share with her children. The fruit grows in clusters that makes it easy to gather a small handful at a time so gathering a bountiful supply is rather quick and easy compared to the gathering of some of the other berries or fruits that grow wild. The seed, or pit of the cherry is large enough that it needs to be removed while rendering the fruit into jam or jelly. It is also said that the pit may contain hydro cyanic acid making the seed unsafe to consume. The pits will become harmless after the cooking process but should be discarded anyway.

I have scarcely touched on the gifts that exist at this time of the year. They are many yet each one serves a purpose depending on the state of preparation we have put ourselves in, according to the season.

This being the moon of ripening is only a short period in the cycle of the seasons, a brief moment in the happenings of life within the circle. The berries that we have the opportunity to enjoy are a pleasant gift indeed but they are also a sign of the end of an easier season to live in. If we were dependent upon the gifts of the earth, this would be a time of serious preparation for the days to come. Of course most of us don't depend upon the seasons and what they have to offer for our survival but there is a lesson here. How many, in the world as you know it, do depend on these gifts of life? Is the world made up of only humans? Is it only our security and welfare that we need to look after? Life on earth is made of so much more than just us and what we need or want. Our life is so closely dependent upon all those things, all those other lives, all those seasons and changes that make this world what it is, all the gifts of life that make life possible. Whether we would like to accept it or not, we are not independent of the rest of the earth, or the miracles of life, or the cycles and the changes that take place within the life of the earth. We are as dependent upon those things as we ever have been. Our lifestyles, opinions and attitudes have helped us to distance ourselves from the reality of life as a whole but it is still whole. One cannot live without all the others and it takes all of the others so that one may live.

SEPTEMBER

⌘

The name September was derived from the Latin word meaning seven since this was the seventh month of the Roman calendar which began in March and had ten months in the year.

On our current calendar, September is the ninth month, I suppose a small oversight in mans effort to accurately record the passing of time. To the Algonquin people, this is the moon of the middle between harvest and eating corn. To many of the people of western North America, this is the moon of drying grass or the moon of colored leaves. To anyone that is aware and observant of the cycles of nature, this is a time of change, of endings and beginnings in our continuing journey along the great circle.

Since the summer solstice that took place in June, our period of daylight in the northern hemisphere has been growing shorter. The diminishing length of daylight is almost imperceptible at first. Gradually we begin to notice as we conduct our busy lives by the hand of the clock that darkness is falling around us a little quicker than before. As we count the days of September, we reach the twenty third day on which falls the autumnal equinox, the second time of the year when daylight and darkness are of equal length. The sun makes its appearance each morning a little further south on the horizon and now the days will become increasingly shorter until the winter solstice in December.

This accelerated rate of diminishing daylight is part of the magic of autumn. Summer has ended and the fall season begins. Again the children of Mother Nature are in fervent anticipation of insuring the survival of their kind and preparing for the trying times of the season ahead.

The magic comes earlier up here in the Rocky Mountains than it does at lower elevations. The landscape puts on a different face as the leaves of the aspen trees turn from green to the brilliant colors of autumn. The mountains become a mosaic of bright yellow and the glowing reds and oranges of the aspens that blend with the various shades of green from the surrounding evergreens and a scattering of white from the early snow that caps the mountain peaks. The morning clouds hover closer to the ground as they slowly drift and meander through the valleys and gently caress the mountains as if they want to share in the glory of the land. As the sun rises higher and the air warms, the wispy, changing figures seem reluctant to rise and break their communion with the earth.

During these fall days, especially in the mornings, you can hear the mystic call of the bull elk in his attempt to attract females or to challenge another bull to a duel. To see a bull elk at this time in his life is truly inspiring. To watch this powerful and magnificent animal as he carries himself so proudly, lifts his nose to the sky with his antlers gracing the length of his back so his voice can be carried to the four winds and sings his ageless song is a humbling experience indeed.

The groups of bull elk that have spent the summer together, sharing their feeding grounds with each other, bedding down and traveling together have now broken up. They are now prepared to do battle with each other to claim dominance over their harems of cow elk. Each one is determined to pass on his heredity to the next generation, to do his part in the continuing survival of his species, to contribute to the circle of life. This annual battling of comrades is just one of the many checks and balances that nature has put in place to make sure the genetic values of the strong are passed on. Although the females make the choice of who to be with, the victor of the seasons challenge is the one they choose. The generations that follow will continue to be an icon of the rugged mountain west.

Here in the Rockies, the warm season is short and always I am amazed at how well our friends of the plant community thrive in these harsh conditions. They have such a short time to complete their cycle from spring sprouting to flowering and going to seed but they seem to realize their task and perform it so well. During the early part of this month I took a small group of people on a three day survival camp in the mountains. Because of the extremely dry conditions this year, Colorado experiencing the worst drought conditions in decades, our chances of finding food and adequate shelter material was a concern that was shared by my students. Since we all carried with us only about a quart of water, it was an immediate priority to find a good, safe place with a water supply to live on for the next three days. As we wandered up a serene little valley, we followed a tributary of Pole creek. The creek itself was very low and actually dried up before it reached its confluence with the Fraser river, but as we reached its source there was still a trickle of life, and close to it grew most of the gifts that would sustain us. There close to the creek where it was moist and shady and we found many of our friends that would help keep us comfortable for the short time that we spent with them. There was Twisted stalk, *Streptopus amplexifolius*, growing right along the edge of what was left of this little mountain stream, also known as the cucumber plant because of its unique flavor that tastes like a blend of watermelon and cucumber. At this time of year the stalks are tough and stringy so we gathered a few and scraped the inner pith out of the stalks which lends itself well with other foods. The berries were also on at this time so we had a little taste of the sweetness of Mother Earth. Although Twisted Stalk is a fine edible, the berries and parts of the mature plant need to be used in moderation since it can be a powerful laxative.

Scattered in patches along the creek bottom was another friend that had much to offer, Cow Parsnip, or *Heracleum Lanatum.* This large, almost tropical looking member of the parsley family always grows in moist areas. Cow Parsnip has a flavor that doesn't appeal to some folks but I like it and all the people on this particular trip seemed to like it also. Commonly, Cow Parsnip is gathered in the spring when the stalks are young and tender but in September they are mature and have produced their seed clusters at the top of the stalk. Again we gathered some of the smaller stalks and peeled the inner pith from the inside. The leaf stalks can be burned to produce a salt substitute to go along with the dried seeds of Field pennycress or Shepherds purse that can be used as pepper. There was a patch of these big plant brothers close to our camp that had been used for a bed by a couple of moose. Since they had all been broken down, one of my students used the large leaves to form shingles over his shelter and the downed stalks to weave between the frame and the leaves. He ended up with a fine shelter that kept him dry and comfortable through a night of rain.

In our quest for food, finding edible plants growing in the low protected areas close to the creek was not difficult but finding them in abundance was. We had to be so very careful and selective in our gathering so that we didn't make a negative impact on the small, struggling groups of plants we found. Because it had been so dry, just a few steps away from the creek bottom there were some of the same plants we wanted to collect but they were stunted and had produced very few seeds so we left them to continue their struggle for life. We were not there to learn how to live off of the land but rather how to live with it, to be a part of it. To share ourselves with nature means not only to look after our own needs but also to be aware of the needs of those that share their lives with us. We need to not be takers but to be caretakers. After our three short days, we prepared to leave. Our surroundings had become familiar, there was a sense of reluctance to leave. The small plant communities we had found were still healthy and with the next rain or breath of the wind, all sign of our being there would vanish. We left knowing that the friends we made were still there and their life struggles would go on as would ours. For a short time we had lived on so little yet we had been given so much. We left carrying treasures you can't touch with your hand but are seen in our memories and felt with our heart.

In this fast paced world that we live in, so many of us have become unaware of the connective tissue that bonds us to the earth and the beauty of life as a whole.

There is so much focus on individualism that we lose sight of the big picture. Every form of life eventually comes full circle. It has its beginning and its end but its kind will continue the path along the great circle of life. I suppose that eventually the life of the earth will also come to a full circle, the end of one grand cycle of life. Until then, the many cycles of nature will continue, some of them so great we have not yet discovered them and those so short they go unnoticed.

There are those that form negative opinions about current methods of wildlife and forest management without realizing the effect their ideas could have on the life of the entire population. No one likes to see peoples lives and homes destroyed by forest fires but if you choose to live where most trees don't live past fifty or sixty years and their seeds are propagated by fire, what would seem the likely thing to happen? The cycles of nature are the actions of the earth being alive, they are necessary for all life. I don't mean to sound cold or uncaring about my fellow man, I do care, but I believe we need to be cautious in our actions. Maybe we should not try so much to control the cycles of the life of the earth but try more to understand them and to expect them.

The Earth is our home, our habitat, our life, it provides for us all that we have. We can not just live on this wonderful planet, we must learn again how to live with it.

September Part 2
Changes

One of the great things about life on this planet is that nothing is constant except change. I have only lived here for a half of a century and I have seen many changes take place through the seasons, and the years, and the places I have had the grand opportunity to experience. We all see changes take place as we travel further down the path of life. Some are good and some are not. There are those changes that go beyond our understanding as individuals and those that are definitely beyond the control of mankind. An important fact that I have tried to stress is that we as the whole of the human race are no more important or less important than all the rest of life but we do have the power to make a greater influence on our habitat than any other life form that exists.

In my short life I have seen winters when there was no snow and winters when I had to dig it away from my door so I could leave my lodge. I have seen summers when there was no rain and summers when the rain never seemed to stop. There have been seasons in my life when it seemed there were more plant greens and berries than I and all my wild friends could eat and then seasons when it seemed there was not enough for even the birds. There have been times when my heart has rejoiced over the abundance the earth had given and then times when I have been saddened because of the scarcity that my furred and feathered brothers and sisters had to endure. I can not control it but I understand it and when I watch them in the wild, I feel it.

There is a unique aspect to tracking, whether it is a man or an animal, or the path of the earth. The distance between tracks is not always the same. Sometimes there is a long step and then sometimes a short one, depending on the conditions of the landscape or the physical condition of the one you are tracking. Mother Earth travels through a little different terrain once in a while and she definitely experiences a changing physical condition every now and then so the tracks she leaves are not always evenly spaced.

We try to look back at the old sign and make sense of it so we can predict the path the earth is taking but it doesn't always make sense to us. The sign varies and there are turns in the trail, there are bits of evidence dropped along the way that make the path confusing yet confirm that we are on the right track. There is so much we know about where she has been yet it is so hard to tell exactly where she is going. Sometimes the track that is followed is influenced by the tracker. The tracker might force the one being followed into taking a different path or force them into a move they wouldn't have made had they not been so diligently pursued.

As we look back on the path of the earth, there have been many variations in her path, the climatic changes that have taken place, the difference in the length between climatic changes and dramatic changes in the environment. Some of those changes have taken place because of forces that are far beyond the presence of mankind and then some of them might be just because of the influence we have on our earth home. I do not believe that mankind can completely change the cycles of the life of the earth but we very well may have an influence upon the length, duration or the sequence of some of those circles in which we live. Our presence and the way we take advantage of those gifts we have discovered may also have a bearing on the period of time that passes between those cycles and what the following generations will have to endure.

There are effects on the earth that mankind has taken the blame for creating, but did we create anything or just influence the way in which it happens? One of the global conditions that we seem to take credit for is global warming. We treat this as some kind of a catastrophe like it has never happened before, but it has. Global warming has been a part of the life of the earth in ways that still remain a mystery to us. It doesn't seem to happen on a regular or systematic time frame but through a very long cycle, it will eventually happen again. What has caused it to happen in the past has been, as far as we can tell, stimulated by natural forces far beyond any life force that has lived on this planet, unless you would consider volcanoes and planetary cycles to be a life force. The way I see it, anything that has an effect on the conditions of life, the changing of our environment and our habitat is a life force. We, the human race, are definitely a powerful life force on this planet. As we continue to look for those things the earth can give to us, do we pursue her so closely that we cause her to make a turn in her trail, to change her step a little or even falter as she moves along her path?

Less than four hundred years ago, those of European persuasion, came to North America to live. They had discovered a new land of promise and hope. It was a discovery only to them because they had never been here before. To the people that already lived here, it was home. According to any theory about how the native people came to live in North America, they have been here for at least fifteen thousand years. They were not hindered by technology or modern convenience or token monetary values. Their lives were directly dependent upon the gifts of the earth. They had spent many generations and made many mistakes to gain this realization. The seed of the grasses was their bread of life, the same as it was to their four legged brothers and sisters that gave them meat. The sun that gave them comfort was the same force that caused the plants to grow. The circle of the seasons kept them vigilant in their way of life as it did with all other things that provided them with life. These people that had lived here for so long lived a much different lifestyle than their new friends from across the ocean. The natives had developed a relationship with the forces of life that was hard for these new people to understand yet it had sustained them for a time so old that their great grandfathers could only remember it as legend, the stories of the people that had been passed down through the generations.

The last four centuries are but a very short time to the earth. For as long as she has been alive, four hundred years is hardly enough time for her to take a breath. Humans are the only living creatures here that have the power of choice. We can choose where and how we live much without the deciding forces of nature. How much of the deciding force of mankind does nature have to try to live with? Thousands of square acres of water are diverted from the pacific watershed to the eastern side of the continental divide every year and still there is not enough water to serve the people. Increased nitrogen levels in polluted air are drifting across the Rocky Mountains from the east that could be harmful to the waters, fish and wildlife that live on the western slope. The effects of burning fossil fuels has changed the atmosphere to extents that are not yet fully understood. If you lived on an island and there was food along the shore, would you dig it up and throw the soil in sea until your home was gone, or would you learn to put your garden back in place? Would you wait until all the food along the shore was gone before you started looking for other things to eat or would you realize that your food was becoming scarce before it was all gone? Would you just live along the shore or would you choose to explore the whole island? Life is full of choices, what path do we choose to follow.

The Earth Mother has given us many opportunities, many chances of choice, many avenues of travel. Do we just choose not to follow the right path or are we bound by monetary value and the time it takes to take a different direction, or both?

OCTOBER

⌘

October, the tenth month of the calendar year as we know it bears the name of the eighth month of the ancient Roman calendar. The way in which man accounts for the passing of time has changed much more than the cycles of nature have in the course of mankind. The natives of North America referred to the passing of time as not just a name of the month but as an occurrence within the unbroken circle of the seasons. To those people that grew crops like the eastern Cherokee people, this is the harvest moon. There were also those that lived in areas that could not support crops. The Lakota people saw this time as the moon of falling leaves and the Cree people saw it as the moon when the birds fly south. It makes no difference who we are or where we live or what we call each piece of time, if we are aware of the path we have followed, we can see what may lay ahead.

The tracks we make as we travel the path of life are the signs we leave of a time gone by. Within those tracks lay the history of mankind, the story of our lives and the changes we have made and the cycles we have gone through. Within the circle there are many cycles. With the beginning of each new cycle, the one before it ends and we leave behind the signs of the impacts we have made. Sometimes we can go back and conceal our tracks, we can brush them away, but sometimes we tread heavily on the face of the earth and it takes a long time to heal. As the earth now travels along the great circle, she bears the scars of abuse across her face but she is a good mother and still provides the needs for life, even to those that have forgotten the relationship they share with her.

As time goes on, our numbers grow and there are more people on the face of the earth now than there ever have been so we leave a much deeper track than we ever have before. We need to tread more lightly, the sign we leave is not so easily erased and we make an enormous impact on the very things that give us life. The size of the track we are leaving is diminishing not only our quality of life, but also those we share it with.

Our ecological footprint is made by how much of the earths resources we consume, how much energy we use and how much space we take up. With current global population in mind, if everyone was to have their fair share of space to provide for all their needs, each person would have to rely on about six acres for all the gifts of life. If we were to share a meager twelve percent of the earths land surface with all other living things that need it, that would leave each one of us about five acres to live on.

As Americans of today, we use on the average, about thirty acres for each one of us. Although we provide many resources, products and food to our fellow humans throughout the world, we still live excessively.

As individuals we consume more, throw away more and use more space doing it than any other culture on the face of the earth. In some northeastern states, there is no space left for garbage. People are forced to recycle and household waste has to be shipped elsewhere to take up more space. I always teach my students of survival to look at their back trail often. Things look different when you see where you have been, it gives you some perspective on the direction you are going. If you have traveled a difficult path, you may not want to go that way again and in the future you will avoid making the same mistake.

Whether you ponder the cycles of nature or those of mankind, sometimes history has a way of repeating itself. Looking back at all the great things we have accomplished as human beings and also at the mistakes we have made, we certainly have the power to choose the path we follow. The burden of choosing the path does not lay just on the shoulders of state and governmental agencies to decide what we use, how much we use or where to put the leftovers, it begins with each one of us. How much do we really need and how can we better use what we have? How can we find a way to give back to the earth for all that she gives us? A little bit of knowledge goes a long way. If you know just a little of what the earth has to offer in a natural setting, how to gather and use some of the gifts she gives, you realize just how closely you are connected to her. If you have ever been in need of food and shelter in a natural setting and had to rely on what nature provided, you know the truth of the gift. The greater our appreciation is for something, the more we want to care for it.

By this time of the year, the fresh plant foods have grown too mature to be good eating, most of the medicinal plants have gone to seed or have completed their growth cycle and are returning to the earth. The people of the past had already prepared for the lean cold months that lay ahead. As the circle of the seasons rolls on, Mother Nature has a way of providing things that we need for that particular time of year. The grasses have become dry and the leaves have fallen to the ground. Since the nights are cooler now, these dried stalks and leaves give us a warm shelter. I have spent many nights outside without a sleeping bag or a tent by using my plant friends to keep me warm. By starting with a simple tripod of sticks a little longer than my body and about three feet high, I stuff it full of dry grass and leaves. After lying down on it to make sure I have a good barrier between the ground and my body, I continue to fill it completely full. After I have a nice cozy nest, I cover the outside of the shelter with more sticks and leaves. By starting at the bottom edge and thatching in the material as I work towards the top it creates a shingle effect that will also keep me dry if it rains or snows. You can also give some life to some dry rocks by heating them in your fire and placing them around the inside edges of your shelter before you get in to sleep. It is easier for your body to keep your shelter warm than to have to warm it. Just be sure your heated rocks are not too hot. I wait until I can pick them up with my hands covered. When you enter your shelter, start feet first and wiggle your feet and legs while easing into it, then pull the thatched lid you have made over the opening and enjoy a warm, cozy nights sleep. Many of the plant friends we use for food and medicine in the warm months become our insulation in the cool months. This is another one of those skills you should practice if you are an outdoors person, it could save your life if for some reason you have one of those unexpected lengthy stays in the woods. This lesson is better learned from the teachers that live by it. Go watch the mice and the squirrels as they build their nests, and listen to them, they speak the language of the heart and it is there you will keep their lesson.

The dried stalks of some plants make excellent cordage and provide us with other ways to obtain food. Fireweed makes a good strong cord and is one of the easiest plants I have found for making cordage . Stinging Nettle also makes a good serviceable cord and Dogbane makes a very strong cord, strong enough to use for a bow string, Any of these will easily make a string quite suitable for setting a snare for a small animal thus gaining a meal, and some self assurance. To make string from a plant you need to first separate the strong outer fibers from the inner stalk. This can be done by flattening the entire stalk and gently bending it or pulling it over a smooth stick to make the dried inner stalk break up so it can be removed from the outer fibers. It helps to dampen the stalk first, this makes the fibers more pliable and easy to work with. Once the fibers have been separated from the stalk you simply twist them together. Start with just twisting the end with your fingers then while holding the twisted end, roll it between the top of your leg and your hand. You now have a cord that you can build a shelter with, mend clothing, replace a shoestring or countless other reasons that you may have for a string, especially in a survival situation. You can also join these strands together to make your cord as long as you need it. Start off center with your first piece and twist it until it wraps around it self, continue this until you are about three or four inches from the shortest end. Mesh the fibers of the end of another single twisted cord with the fibers of one of the ends of the double twisted cord and continue the wrap. By starting off center, you don't have two splices in the same place which produces a strong cord. The simple act of using a part of nature to provide a need can have a profound impact on how we feel about those things we used to consider simpler forms of life. Practicing the skills of living with the Earth helps to keep us aware that all things work together to keep the delicate fabric of life together.

It is amazing, but not beyond comprehension, how wonderfully the intricate workings of nature have been designed. Every need for every thing is met according to the season at hand. Fresh food is laid out before us in the spring when we need it most. The warm months of summer offer us the opportunity to prepare for the future, for the animals to raise their young, for the plants, which are the only producers of food to continue their growth cycle. The fall offers the insulation of dried plants to give us a warm bed. A time when the young are raised so we can accept the gift of meat for food and furs for clothing from the four legged ones without having an adverse effect on their welfare as a whole. Then there comes winter, a time to reflect on our actions, our lives and the gifts we receive and to benefit from the fruits of our preparation.

Certain things take place at certain times for certain reasons. Any time is a good time to look back on the tracks we leave, to try to make sense of the path we follow, to try to find ways we can give back for all we are given and to make the best of what we have which includes the greatest gift of all, life.

The sign of what lays ahead can be found in the tracks we leave.

October Part 2
Going nuts

If you lived in the past and belonged to the people that lived under the harvest moon, your harvest would include much more than the crops you had grown. The eastern parts of the United States have been blessed with many different kinds of nut producing hardwood trees. At this time of the year, these mighty and sometimes ancient trees give us a kind of sustenance that we can't eat, they nourish our spirit. In their preparation for the winter, their metabolism slows down and the production of chlorophyll in the leaves stops and reveals the red and yellow pigments that produce the brilliant colors of fall. This is when many people unintentionally lose track of time and get caught up in the moment. Mother Nature makes her presence known in a way that can not be ignored. The colors of the trees, the texture of the landscape, the crispness of the air, the anticipation of a changing season has a way of capturing your attention. The way the sun reflects from the colors of the leaves as a gentle breeze causes them to wave makes the trees look as if they are themselves, illuminated. As the process of life is suspended, the action of life is made more evident. There is a sense of warmth and tranquility in the coolness of autumn and our spirit is fed, our bond to the earth is made stronger and the beauty of life goes far beyond the moment.

There are also ways in which these old standing ones help feed our bodies. The nuts they produce are called mast and there are many different kinds of flavors and textures to choose from. I still have visions of my Dad, at his workbench, cracking the hulls of hickory nuts and picking the delicious meat from the shell. As long as he was physically able he would spend hours in his shop, gleaning the gift of what we were allowed to pick up from the ground. He was kind of like a kid in a berry patch, he would eat at least as much as he would put in the jar that was kept to share with the family and that indescribable banana hickory nut bread that Mom would bake for the holidays. Those times that I spent with my family gathering what would later be a reminiscent feast, time spent with loved ones and the gifts given by the earth are within me and can never go away.

There are several varieties of hickory nuts. Some are small and difficult to collect very much of the meat while others are larger and much worth the effort it takes to reach those detectible morsels inside the shell. Hickory nuts have a thick hull made up of four sections that protects the shell. Before you can crack the nut you must first remove the hull. When the nuts first drop from the tree, the hull is mostly green and very tightly bound to the shell. If you wait until the ground has been frosted or if they have been on the ground for several days, the hull will turn brown and curl at the points of the sections breaking their adhesion to the shell and are then easily removed. You can also gather the nuts whole and let them sit at home in a bushel basket or even spread out and eventually the hulls will dry out and turn brown and be just as easily removed. If you collect the ones on the ground that have dried out, sometimes the worms will beat you to the nut. They will bore a little hole in the shell that is easy to see before you crack it open. There were times that Dad and I would be cracking open the nut shell and find one of those fat little white grubs. We would put them in a small jar along with some sawdust and nut crumbs and put them in the refrigerator. Later when the ice would form on the lakes we would take those little grubs ice fishing and turn them into a fine mess of Bluegill. Instead of thinking the worms had ruined a nut, we thanked them for giving a much larger gift. Fresh Bluegill, caught through the ice, provides a meal that is more than fit for a king.

Many were the days that found me sitting against the trunk of a hardwood tree, watching the daylight gradually enlighten me to the beginning of another day. Dew drops falling from the trees, the mist rising from the ground, the night dwellers seeking refuge from the day and the day dwellers waking to feed and rest in the warmth of the sun. The stately figures of the tree trunks in the mist and the delicate under story glistening in the cool moistness of a new day always gave me a sense of serenity and humility as I beheld the beauty of nature. Soon, the shy and cautious Fox Squirrel would emerge from its nest, anxious to feed on the newly formed nuts at the tips of the branches of the hickory trees. They would easily peel the hull from the nuts and drop them to the ground, a sound would seem to reverberate through the quiet, early morning woods alerting me to their whereabouts. There were trees that were favorites among the squirrels. Being familiar with these certain trees, I would wait, listen and watch. After a while there would be a gathering of squirrels in the same tree. With so many eyes watching, I would carefully and slowly move from one hiding place to another until I was close to the tree they were in. There, with a small tree to steadily rest my 22 rifle against, I would collect only enough to make a fine meal. I always went prepared to clean my game so I could leave the parts I didn't want in the woods so as to provide a meal to the first birds, opossum or raccoon that would find it. Hickory nuts have provided for me and my family in many ways, one little nut that gives in so many ways.

Another one of the giving trees is the Walnut. The nut produced by the walnut tree is larger than the hickory nut and also has a hull that covers the shell. The hull that covers the walnut is not in sections like the hickory nut. It is a complete covering without any sections or segments but it is much thinner than the hull of a hickory nut. The biggest difference between the walnut and the hickory nut is that the walnut contains a black resin between the hull and the shell. Again the same holds true that if you allow the walnut to age before you try to remove the hull, the hull comes loose from the shell much easier. Once the hull has become darkened it is not hard to grind the nut under foot to loosen the hull. It would be a good idea to wear gloves to pick up the nut shells after you have removed the hulls. The black resin that lines the inside of the hull will stain your fingers and is nearly impossible to wash off.

During my youth while growing up in Indiana, I would be out every fall collecting walnuts. I was not only after the rich flavor of the nut but also the dark resin of the hulls. After removing the hulls from the nut I would boil them in a washtub along with the traps I would spend the rest of the year tending. The walnut hulls would dye my steel traps a dark color and make them easier to conceal and remove any residual human smell they might hold.

Like most of the other nuts, there are more than one variety of walnuts. There is the very common black walnut and also the white walnut which is commonly called the butternut. I once found a basket of butternuts in my parents garage that had been there for so long they had dried up and the nut meat was no longer fit to eat. Because of unfortunate circumstances and the passing of years, these nuts that had once been gathered with anticipation had escaped the memory of those that gathered them. Out of curiosity, I took some of these dried up butternuts and cut the shell into thin slices with my band saw. What developed was a design of nature that was delicate and beautiful, a pattern that resembled a wooden snowflake. I was pleased to discover another work of the creators art, one that could have so easily went unseen.

Acorns, the mast crop of the mighty oak tree, the most ignored and unappreciated source of food is not considered by most folks as a nut to be collected. The acorn has a thin shell and a cap that is easily removed but the nut meat is often bitter and has an astringent taste because of it's high content of tannin. Tannin is an acidic substance that can be easily removed in several ways. The tannin content varies between the several different kinds of oak trees. Oak trees are divided in basically two groups, the red oak which has little spines at the tip of the lobes of the leaves and white oaks in which the leaf spines are absent. The white oak is the one that produces the best tasting acorn. I have gathered acorns from beneath white oak trees and eaten them right there and found them quite good. There is always that slight astringent taste but it is not overbearing. The red oak on the other hand holds a more concentrated tannin content and so are very bitter when eaten raw. Acorns can be boiled in several changes of water to remove the tannin and then dried or roasted in a slow oven to reveal a mild and nut like flavor.

Considering the long and enduring history of mankind on the face of the earth, the acorn has probably provided more meals and sustenance than all of the other nuts and grains now commonly used. Oak trees of various description grow in many parts of the world. They have been used for food as far back as we can trace our existence yet have become almost forgotten, especially in North America. There is more nutrition in a palm full of acorn meal than can be found in a bowl of oatmeal.

The acorn offers more ways in which to use it than any other nut I can think of. It can be eaten raw, especially if it is of the white oak variety or prepared in several different ways. The natives used to crush them and then boil them in water. The nut meat has a tendency to float to the top of the water while the shells would settle to the bottom making it easy to recover the sweet flesh of the acorn for further use. At this stage, the acorn could eaten as is, dried and ground into a meal or added to other foods. The rich brown colored water left over from leaching the tannin out of the nuts was also put to use. Tannin is the main ingredient necessary for tanning hides. The acorn will release enough tannin through the boiling process that skins can be soaked in the left over water to be tanned with the golden hue that we associate with buckskin leather.

I have only mentioned a very few of the nut bearing trees yet the gifts are many. When we explore the ways in which our natural friends provide for us we don't always look past the obvious. Sometimes there is so much more than just food or medicine. The trees, the ancient ones, feed our bodies, they feed our souls. Since the beginning of civilization, they have even made easier our task of living.

The next time you go out to gather the gifts of the earth, remember there is more than meets the eye, or the mouth. It is the fruit of the spirit that strikes a rhythm and gives harmony to life.

NOVEMBER

⌘

Our manner of knowing where we are in the course of a year is important yet the labels we have chosen to remind us of our place along the giant path seem somewhat out of place. The name, November does not correspond with the fragment of time we have placed it in. The names of the last four months of the modern calendar represent the numbers of those months according to the ancient ten month Roman calendar. November is derived from the word, *novem*, meaning nine yet we know it as the eleventh month of the year. The Anglo-Saxon people called this month *Blodmonath* which meant blood-month and was the time for slaughtering cattle, an annual act of preparation for the coming winter. The people of the Lakhota nation called this time *wani-cokan-wi,* the moon of starting winter which told them the final preparations made to sustain them through trying times should be done. For those that lived with the earth, the Earth Mother was the one that named the month. It was nature that proclaimed the circle of the seasons, the place on the path of our journey around the sun. It was the signs of nature that said where we should be in our state of preparing to live with what was coming. It was this need for preparation and a deep respect for the powers of nature that created a harmonious balance between nature and man.

During this month, there is a much celebrated holiday among the citizens of the United States of America, Thanksgiving. After the first colony of pilgrims in Plymouth had survived a winter that had tested their fortitude and their will to live, another season came to pass. As the grain ripened in the fields and the squash and pumpkins swelled to maturity, they gathered their crops for another winter. This was the year of 1621. William Bradford, the Governor of the Plymouth colony proclaimed a day of thanksgiving which resulted in a three day feast among the pilgrims and their newly acquired Native American friends. The survivors of the first winter had learned many lessons about this new land they now occupied, and they were fortunate indeed to have made friends with the natives that had so much to teach them. This was a land of plenty, a paradise of game and upland birds that filled the woods and prairies. In the fall the rivers brimmed with thousands of vibrant, spawning Atlantic Salmon and the land was rich with edible and medicinal plants. Most of these birds and animals and plants were unknown to these new people but under the tutelage of the native Americans, these new things became the friends and sustenance of the pilgrims.

These people that had traveled across a turbulent ocean to this new land of freedom had been given many gifts of knowledge from those that had raised many generations in this place. A friendship had been formed between these very different kinds of people but that relationship would soon be swallowed up and lost in the conflicting views of their relationship with the land. The pilgrims had enjoyed a profitable beaver trade with the Indians that they used to pay their debts to England. By 1640, the fur trade declined due to the French trappers in the north and competition for furs in the Connecticut River valley by people from the Massachusetts Bay colony. The men of Plymouth then began to claim ownership of parcels of land for profit and deny the Indians access to what had long been their hunting grounds. It became obvious to the Wampanoag people and other tribes in the area that these new people did not intend to share the land but to control it. In 1675, the remaining people of the Wampanoag tribe that had not died from smallpox and other diseases began their effort to regain the paradise their grandfathers had found so long ago. The Wampanoag people were joined by the Narragansett and the Nipmuck in a fight to save the small part of the earth they belonged to but they were outnumbered by the colonial army. By 1678 the once simple and colorful way of life of the native people of the north east coast had become only an image of the past.

There is a much larger picture here than the changing of the lives of people, a partnership between man and nature had been broken. A culture that had thrived for thousands of years on deep respect and sincere gratitude for the gifts of nature had been given over to those that viewed these gifts as theirs for the taking. It seemed this new land held a never ending supply of food and medicine to fill the needs of these new Americans. If only they had listened more closely to those that had already learned the need to share with the land, to give back what they could, to care for that which cared for them. A time would come when a few of these new Americans would realize the need of appreciation for the gifts of life, that giving back was not always a physical act but sometimes an act of humility, a giving of the self, an attitude of the heart. The insight of the few although overshadowed by the greedy majority would eventually have an impact on the future of the wildlife and habitat, but not without some shortsighted actions to begin with.

In 1630, only a decade after their arrival to this new land, the Massachusetts Bay colony established a one penny bounty on wolves due to their mythical fear of the predator and ignorance of it's role within the natural community. With the wolf population reduced, the white-tailed deer which adapted well to the crop lands developed by the settlers flourished. With the ease of harvesting the deer that frequented the edges of the pilgrims crops, they too were soon reduced to scarcity which led to a closed hunting season for the deer on Rhode Island in 1646. These attempts at wildlife management, to insure the fair share of a renewable resource continued for many years but were poorly regulated since they were so locally oriented.

The idea of wildlife management was not a new concept born in the minds of these new Americans. Having an active role in caring for this planetary garden is inherent to mankind. In the Bible, Moses wrote in Deuteronomy, 22 - 6, "If you come across a birds nest beside the road, either in a tree or on the ground, and the mother is sitting on the young or on the eggs, do not take the mother with the young. You may take the young, but be sure to let the mother go, so that it may go well with you and you may have a long life."

By seventeen hundred, the human population of European settlers along the Atlantic coast had grown into the millions. By 1708, many hunting regulations were in place and New York had established seasons on upland game birds, all a lifetime away from the United States gaining their independence from British rule. These new Americans did not come here with the intention of decimating the wildlife or destroying the habitat, they only sought the freedom to live a way in which they believed in. The rapid growth, greed and ignorance that followed was the faltering step in our caring for a precious gift. The settlers had landed on the edge of a place that stretched beyond their dreams, a land more vast than they could even imagine. In a short 200 years, this expanse of land that connected two oceans had gone from an era of abundance and the excitement of exploration to a period of overexploitation and the decimation of wildlife. By 1900, the beaver which had been the driving economical force of a nation had been reduced to a rare encounter across the country. The magnificent, noble wild turkey that had almost won its place as our national emblem had been erased from all of its original range except for a few isolated pockets in the Ozarks of Missouri. The extremely adaptable and versatile white tailed deer had been nearly removed from existence. The more than ten million bison that once roamed the vast prairies of the west, the life blood of the wonderfully proud and powerful people that lived there, were near extinction.

The Earth Mother has sacrificed so much for the progress of mankind, much of the harmony between man and nature is gone and a new balance needs to be found. We have learned so much from our mistakes and from the lessons our four legged and winged brothers and sisters have shown us. We know now that the environmental quality of our land involves so much more than single areas or specific populations. We know that the land and all that lives on it and in it are connected, the cycles of life involves all life because each life makes an impact on all others.

When it comes to managing our environment , we have learned that there is a time for preservation, a time for conservation, a need for diversity, a time to accept the gifts of a renewable resource. Everyone can help the environment through responsible individual choices, but not everyone can make the right decisions when it comes to managing our habitat, it takes years of research and learning and dedication to the desire to do it right. When we make decisions about things we don't fully understand, reality becomes clouded by emotion and we choose what makes us feel better instead of facing the reality of the best decision. To this day, the growing numbers of mankind are still encroaching on the habitat, nature is disappearing at an alarming rate from natural and pristine areas of North America to the rain forests of the Amazon basin. We can not change this trend by saving a deer from being hunted or a beaver from being trapped or a tree from being cut down. You can not look at one part of the natural realm as being more important than another, it takes all of the parts together to equal one. One earth is all we have to live on and our lives depend on the awesome diversity of this planet. For so long, people from all ages and cultures have lived in specialized societies, each person making their own contribution to the good of the whole. We each have talents, skills and educations that provide not only for ourselves but also provide a service to the many. So it is with the management of our natural resources. There are those that have dedicated their lives to this profession because that is where their passions lie. Their job should not be interfered with by a popular vote or the throws of single minded activists. We the people adopted the public trust doctrine to insure that our lands and waters will remain for us all and that those we choose to manage them for the good of the people could do so. We need to allow them to make intelligent, realistic decisions based on sound research and education concerning the management of what is left of nature. In the long run, we will not be able to eat, drink or breathe money and the grand cycles of life will not be governed by our emotions alone.

Our love and compassion for all life joined with the acceptance of the harsh realities of the natural world can help us appreciate the richness of life, to be a part of the whole, to take much care in the way we receive the many gifts of life. Whenever you engage in outdoor activities, you enter in to the natural world, you become a participant in the circle of life. When enough of us become aware of our actions as individuals, it becomes an enormous group effort for the good of the whole. The good you do, you do for us all.

November Part 2
Choices

⌘

In a time past, not so long ago, North America was inhabited by people of different tribes, different languages, different ideas of personal beauty and wealth yet they shared many common ethical and moral standards. The natives of North America, although sometimes separated by cultural idiosyncrasies, lived according to the gifts they received and the efforts they put forth in order to provide for their people. Whether they were the kind of people that grew crops or were hunters and gatherers, they all relied upon what the earth gave them and there was much gratitude in what they received. They had learned through the centuries that what gave them life was not to be taken for granted. It took hard work and dedication to the family and the community to insure the survival of their kind. They earned their living by recognizing how to process those things that were made possible by nature to give them life. They were well aware of the simple fact that it took life to give life. It made no difference whether they dug a root from the ground, plucked a stem and leaves from the place it had grown or drew the blood of a breathing animal. They knew that all things are part of the great circle of life, that all things follow the same giant path. The plant food, medicine, meat, clothing and shelter were all made possible by the giving and the taking of life.

The disputes that took place between these people were not over how the other lived but rather where they were. These people sometimes relied upon the same area to hunt for the meat or collect the furs and skins that were essential for their survival. Sometimes the journey of different tribes would overlap in their quest for the same thing yet seldom was there the taking of a human life. In those days, among the American natives, there was no war over the difference of opinion, religion or race, only the effort of each one to gain what was needed to live.

When Europeans first came to this land of promise, they too were in search of the necessities of life. As humans, our lives are in need of more than food, shelter and clothing. Our reward for living does not come from simply following the path we are on, the reward is in how we make our journey. The pilgrims came to America with the hope of freedom, the chance to live their lives as they saw fit. The ability to live according to their religious convictions, to decide for themselves the ethical and moral standards they believed in were essential to their quality of life. In the short history of the United States of America, the ideology of individualism is one of the things that has made this country such a great place to live in but in recent years it seems that some of us have had our ethical choices put to the challenge. We all have standards that we choose to live by and we believe in them because we perceive them to be true. Our ethics are based on our personal judgment of what we perceive to be the truth and by our nature, we associate ourselves with others that share the same ideas of moral conduct. Our idea of what is ethical is what directs us to join with people of similar interests whether it is a religious organization, a business association or a special interest group.

In the last several years, the number of special interest groups that have formed and the money and effort they put into voicing their opinion is phenomenal. I guess you could say that I belong to one of these groups because I am an outdoor enthusiast, I like to hunt and fish. The picture that has been formed in the minds of many is that a hunter is an egotistical maniac with a lust for blood. This couldn't be further from the truth. Sure, there are those people that commit acts of brutality, take lives without conscience and kill animals out of season or just for the trophy but these people are not hunters. I am a hunter and I do not consider myself in any way associated with people that have such a lack of ethical or moral convictions.

Hunting today is not what it was in the past. There used to be a time when hunting was an act of survival , a seasonal part of the life of the people. It was a time of making sure you were worthy of the gift, a time of praying and giving gratitude to those things that made life possible. A time of humility because you understood that your life and those you loved were dependent upon what you received. It was a time of taking, but not without transgression. More importantly, it was a time to understand what had been given.

In the last four hundred years, the word hunting has been associated with many different actions and mentalities. In the 1600s, people killed wolves for a one penny bounty, then they killed deer that hovered at the edge of their newly planted fields of crops. That was called hunting, but was it really hunting or just collecting another part of the crop? As westward expansion took place and people moved further toward the Mississippi valley, hunting was a way of making money by delivering meat to the settlers. Then the government officials in Washington decided that the best way to discourage the natives from their traditional way of life was to kill off the buffalo. If there were no bison for the natives to live on, they would eventually die off. With that there came the famous buffalo hunts from the windows of trains. America was well on it's way to entering the same state of depraved natural conditions that the pilgrims had left for a land of hope and promise.

By 1900, it became obvious that the future of America and what made this country so special could not continue along the path it followed. Natural areas and the wildlife that made this large island unique from any other place on earth needed to be saved from shallow thinking and greed. The people that stepped forward as advocates for the natural realm, to save the land and its inhabitants from a dismal and empty future were none other than people that called themselves, hunters. These people had spent much of their time in natural surroundings. Through their own observation and participation in the ways of nature, they had gained an intimate sense of what life was really like for those that called the woods and prairies their home.

Because of people like John Muir, Gifford Pinchot, Theodore Roosevelt, Aldo Leopold and J.N. Ding Darling, there were acts of congress that took place and policies established for the protection and management of wildlife. The Forest Service was made to manage the woodlands for more than just timber. National parks, wildlife refuges and the protection of wetlands came into being. Each year, billions of dollars are needed to support the agencies, the people within them and the countless hours of research and study needed to try to provide quality of living for those that live in the wild. Where does all of this money come from? To put it in a nut shell, hunters and fisherman that buy license and equipment.

Today's hunters are of a different breed than in the past. They are the kind of people that are concerned for the future and share a love for wild places. They are the last ones in the world that want to see animal populations decimated or habitats destroyed. The hunt is not so much for the kill as it is for the experience of participating with life. A true hunter realizes that regulations placed on hunting are not to restrict him or her but to insure the future of the wildlife. The kill is the least important thing of the hunt. What is important is the quality of life it provides. Some of my most cherished memories are from times I have spent with my father while hunting, the lessons I have learned about the reality of life and the gratitude I have gained for all that it takes just for me to exist.

When you assume the role of a predator, you move and act differently than you would if you were just taking a hike in the woods. You see things with a different perspective, you observe things that you would never see any other way. You learn things that the casual passer by will never know. Your awareness level is heightened and your instincts come alive and you not only see and hear your surroundings, you feel it. What true hunters get from the hunt is impossible to explain to one that has never had the experience. Hunters are not only necessary for the proper management of wildlife, they are responsible for the flourishing populations of animals we enjoy today.

As Americans, we enjoy many forms of freedom, one being responsible ethical choices. Our quality of living is directly dependent upon the ethical and moral standards we choose to live by. Some of us go to church, some of us don't. Some of us choose to hunt and some of us don't. These are choices we make for ourselves, this is how we choose to make our journey.

DECEMBER

⌘

December, the last month according to the modern calendar, the end of a cycle of time, the final track of another year as we continue along our path. To the Lakhota people, this is the moon of middle winter. An elder is sitting by the flickering light of the fire in the center of his lodge. He is painting the only recorded history of his people. In the pictures on the tanned hide before him are the stories of his tribe called the winter count. There are stories of good hunts and brave warriors, children coming to be and elders going away, stories of gifts received and sacrifices made, a history of the cycle of life within the tribe. These are the stories the children will be told about their people, this is how they will know who they are and the path their people have followed. We all have a history, it is our heritage, our culture, our tool to learn from. Our history of America today is rich with culture and diversity, full of triumph and tragedy. It abounds with lessons about appreciation and acceptance of our fellow man and our environment and should tell us about the role we play beyond the streets and the parking lots.

What makes life interesting is change, a cycle is only the process of something changing. Sometimes if a cycle continues long enough it will eventually go full circle to a place it has previously been. During this month there is a specific point in a natural cycle that we can see, the winter solstice. Since the autumnal equinox in September, the period of daylight each day has grown shorter until we reach the shortest day of the year in the northern hemisphere. On the 21st, sometimes the 22nd day of this month, the northern half of the earth is tilted to its furthest point away from the sun. Our journey has brought us again to a place halfway between autumn and spring so the end of our calendar year can easily be recognized as, the moon of middle winter.

The orbit of the earth around the sun is not a perfect circle. Although the northern hemisphere of the earth is now tilted to its furthest point away from the sun, in about two weeks the earths' orbit will bring it to its closest point to the sun, a place in the path of the earth called perihelion. This point closest to the sun will regress about one day every 58 years and will complete a cycle in about 21,000 years. The wobble of the earth on its axis called lunisolar precession will cause the north star to change many times over a period of about 26,000 years. The angle of the earths tilt will go from 22.1 degrees to 24.5 degrees compared to its current 23.45 degrees through a cycle called obliqity that will take 42,000 years to complete. The shape of the earths orbit which is now nearly a perfect circle will also change. There is now about 6% difference between our closest point to the sun and our furthest point which consists of about 3,000,000 miles and will change to about a 30% difference in a cycle that takes 95,000 years to go full circle. There will be vast differences in the climate of the earth that we will never see as individuals. The changes to our environment that we notice in our lifetimes are due mostly to the actions of mankind through increased human population, habitat destruction and the ill effects of misguided groups and individuals. The grand cycles of the life of the earth have been cast into place by powers far greater than ourselves. There is no wisdom or knowledge possessed in the whole of mankind that can change, manipulate or control them, yet knowledge is a good thing. The scientific community has drawn us a map of the future so that we can carefully choose the path we follow now.

People have lived on this planet for many thousands of years and have flourished amid the many changes in their climate and atmosphere. We have learned how to use many gifts but, have we become greedy ? We have learned how to alter our environment to favor ourselves, but have we forgotten those we share it with ? We have the ability to see not into our immediate future but into that of the generations yet to come, are we now building a past that the future can live with ?

Mankind has traveled a path with many turns and we now stand at a junction we have never seen. The density of human population has crossed over local thresholds and has become a global issue. In July, I mentioned the Hohokam people that had turned their desert environment into a lush and comfortable place to live. The ingenuity of these people allowed them to remain in their home for approximately 900 years but being a creature of nature, they were subject to the inevitable workings of nature. With an increased food supply came an accelerated growth in population until finally they had outgrown their resources. A long history of an elaborate culture that had grown from determination collapsed. The piece of earth they lived on became to exhausted to support them any longer and they abandoned their homes.

No longer are we afforded the choice to move on to an uninhabited land. Each time overpopulation has reached a critical level, man has found relief through invention. Breakthroughs in agricultural practices and genetic engineering have increased the food supply. Technological developments have made more efficient use of our energy resources, but the earth will not grow any bigger and the carrying capacity of our habitat could eventually reach its limits. In the last 50 years, 3 billion acres of soil, an area large enough to equal India and China combined, have been rendered useless for growing crops. Over 42 million acres of tropical rain forest was destroyed in the 1980s alone. Many countries are facing severe water shortages and some fish populations in the oceans have been depleted almost beyond recovery. These are sobering and unpleasant things to think about but reality is not always pretty to look at. Knowing these things should certainly make us even more grateful for the gifts of life, the elements of the earth that make life possible and the grand and wondrous places that still exist.

While standing in a high place and looking out across the rugged beauty of the rocky mountains, sitting along a stream in the cool shade of the Appalachians or canoeing on a peaceful and pristine lake in the north woods, it is hard to imagine the suffering of the earth. We can not see with our eyes the increased levels of carbon dioxide in the atmosphere or the phosphorus and nitrogen concentrations in the oceans. The effects of human population on this planet are sometimes quite obvious and sometimes very well hidden. There are different opinions about the future of mankind, whether we will breed ourselves into extinction or choose a different path. I believe, I hope, that we are again realizing our dependence on the earth, the care it deserves from us and the need to maintain the awesome diversity of life that we share.

Being active members of the community of life involves so much more than the human population. Our survival depends on more than just providing food and shelter for ourselves. Our lives, and especially the quality of our lives is tightly bound to everything on earth. In the realm of nature there is nothing insignificant or without purpose. Everything, living and nonliving contributes to the biochemical cycles necessary for life to exist. We, being the stewards of the earth hold in our grasp the ability to make a difference. The path we follow will be the one we choose. Will we pass on our inheritance or give it away to greed and ignorance?

Our future does not hinge entirely on what has already been done and definitely not on the assumption that we will continue along the same trail that those before us have followed. The difference we make will be in what we do now and how we act in the future. We need to accept what the Earth Mother does while she carries on with the task of living. Sometimes a forest must burn to keep itself healthy and rejuvenate the habitat for those that live there. A river needs to occasionally swell and purge its course to cleanse itself of silt and debris. Sometimes the earth takes a deep breath and exhales those gale force winds that have disastrous effects on peoples lives but to the earth they are just a natural occurrence, a function of the body of the earth. There are those things, those powerful workings of nature of which our presence holds no consequence yet often there are times we should participate with nature and be an integral part of the cycles of life. The forest service is made up of people that can skillfully assist with burning the understory of a forest to help protect the sanctity of life for those of us that have the opportunity to live there. Our feathered and four legged brothers and sisters are confined to the only places to live that have been left for them. Our presence has driven off the more solitary ones, the predators, that worked to keep harmony and balance within their place of living. There is a void we have created and so must responsibly fill. Whether we are gathering herbs, picking mushrooms, hunting or fishing, we need to define the difference between what we can really use and what we want to take home. Some plants live within a delicate, fragile existence while others may benefit from our use of their gifts. Some animals are in the situation to outgrow their comfortable living conditions and ruin their very place of living simply through the act of survival, they too have a gift to give. Responsible land use is the obligation of everyone that enjoys the outdoors. The impacts we make and the tracks we leave are evidence of the compassion, or the lack of it, that we have for the earth and the kinship we share with her. The sign we leave behind will show clearly the ethical standards we adhere to and our actions will make a far deeper impression than our words.

If today, we were to take a look at our winter count, who are we? What kind of path have our people followed and what have we learned along our journey? When we look beyond the confines of our own life to see what it takes for us to live, we should be grateful for all of the gifts, careful of the way we go and anxious to participate in the cycle of life.

Within the great circle of life there are many circles, big circles, little ones, circles within circles. Through the generations of mankind we have watched many of these cycles completed, cycles in the life of the earth and cycles of life on earth. We have learned a little about the awesome and wondrous diversity of life on this planet as it speeds through space on journeys we will share only a short part of. As we continue on our journey, may we learn more and become better at fulfilling our duties as the CARETAKERS.

December Part 2
The moment

We live in a changing world, a world that is still being shaped and molded. Our home is not exactly the way it was yesterday and will be slightly different tomorrow. The giant Redwoods of northern California have spent thousands of years growing to become what they are today but each day they change just a little. They add to their stature, grow a little older and the life forms that they support go through their own tiny cycles. The Canyon Lands of Utah have not spent the last hundreds of thousands or millions of years forming into the awe inspiring mosaic of deep canyons and high plateaus to stop where they are today. The oceans, the mountains, the rivers and the plains are all changing. The earth is a work in progress, a living, breathing, on going form of art that goes beyond the bounds of the most imaginative mind. We see things as they are in just this moment that is our life.

In just the last couple of centuries, man has become aware of the many changes that take place while the earth lives. Our current place of residence doesn't seem as safe as it did a century or two ago. There was a time when a person could go in search of a place that held the promise of a new life, new hope, the anticipation of a better future and room to grow. There were settlers and mountain men that lived a life of solitude and tranquility at the same time they struggled with the everyday task of surviving. To them, the future was endless and the land held more than they could use, but life did not go on without sacrifice.

Recently, my wife and I visited the Arches national park in Utah. There is an old settlement cabin there that was built by a man in the late 1800s. He lived there until 1913 with his daughter and her husband and their two children in a ten by thirteen foot cabin built out of cedar and pinion pine from the desert. They raised cattle and traveled to the nearby town of Moab to order their supplies. They taught their children, tended their cattle and collected their water and firewood and maintained their home in a desolate desert environment. This wouldn't be the kind of life that most of us would choose these days but it was their choice. They were surrounded by the beauty and wonders that today we have to pay money just to look at. They lived their life according to the way they chose, unhindered by what went on in the rest of the world and secure in just providing the needs of life.

Today life is much different than it was a century or two ago. With global communication we know about what happens in the rest of the world. Now we see the devastation, destruction and the havoc that is displayed in peoples lives because of the way the earth lives. Some of us are worried about what will happen to us because of where we live. We are aware of the tectonic plates under the surface of the land and why they cause earthquakes. We know about the controlling forces that make volcanoes erupt. What we don't know is when these things will happen. The earth lives by the way she feels and she reacts to what she feels inside. Are we so different from the way she is?

Of when we are born, we have no recollection, when we will die we can't foresee, what we do in the middle is who we are. There is much to be said about living in the moment. In the moment there is no past and there is no future, there is only now. When I talk to the plants of whom I wish a gift, There is no thought of yesterday or tomorrow, only now. When I look for a gift from my four legged brother or sister, my mind is not on anything but the moment in which we both are together and alive. The ending of one only means the continuation of the other. That is the circle of life, my circle of life. I do not take any life lightly or selfishly but with much thanksgiving. I know that all life is combined into the same circle. Nothing goes away, it just goes another way. A gift is not a gift until it has been received.

I have spent my life hunting, trapping, fishing and gathering. I have learned to follow the mysteries that would have gone unnoticed had I not read the sign. I have gathered gifts from the bark of trees, the flesh of my four legged brothers and sisters, the fruit and roots of the plant people and those that swim yet I have learned that I can give back as much if not more than I take. The hardest lesson to learn is, should I accept this gift or am I allowed to take it? The ancient language of the heart is still alive and all of life knows how to speak it. All we have to do is remember to ask and learn how to listen and do our best to take care of what we have.

Medicine Walker

About the Author

⌘

    Jodie Boxell was born and raised in the small community of Hartford City Indiana. He was raised by parents that lived according to strict religious standards that didn't allow their children to participate in social events. Without the usual things that kept young people entertained in the 1960s, Jodie turned to the woods that were close to his home. The outdoors became more to him than just an escape from the confinement of his parents house, it became his refuge, his release and he made friends there that would remain with him for the rest of his life.

By the time he was ten years old, he tended his own trapline, early every morning before school. At the age of thirteen, his father took him on a fly in fishing trip to Canada where he became more enthralled with the differences in the land, the length of daylight in another place and the quiet and serenity of the north woods. It was a turning point in his life and he became dedicated to learning all he could about what the earth has to offer, how he could better live with it and how he could return the favor of life. The animals, the birds, the trees, plants and even the wind became his family, his teachers and those he knew he had to learn to live with.

Jodie was given the name Medicine Walker at the Silver Bear mountain man rendezvous in 1999. He has taught survival and wilderness skills classes for many years in Colorado. He is a member of the Grand County Search & Rescue team and has a wife and children that share his respect for the earth. This book is only the continuation of a much longer journey.